Microsoft®

Exploring

PowerPoint® 2002

Chapters 3 and 4

Microsoft®

Exploring

PowerPoint® 2002

Chapters 3 and 4

Robert T. Grauer Maryann Barber

University of Miami *University of Miami*

Prentice
Hall

PRENTICE HALL *Upper Saddle River, New Jersey 07458*

Senior Acquisitions Editor: Jodi McPherson
VP/Publisher: Natalie Anderson
Managing Editor: Eileen Clark
Assistant Editor: Kerri Limpert
Editorial Assistant: Maryann Broadnax
Technical Editor: Cecil Yarbrough
Media Project Manager: Cathleen Profitko
Marketing Assistant: Jason Smith
Production Manager: Gail Steier deAcevedo
Project Manager: Lynne Breitfeller
Production Editor: Greg Hubit
Associate Director, Manufacturing: Vincent Scelta
Manufacturing Buyer: Lynne Breitfeller
Design Manager: Pat Smythe
Interior Design: Jill Yutkowitz
Cover Design: Blair Brown
Cover Illustration: Marjorie Dressler
Composition: GTS
Printer/Binder: Banta Menasha

10 9 8 7 6 5 4 3 2 1
ISBN 0-13-140736-8

To Marion —
my wife, my lover, and my best friend

Robert Grauer

To Frank —
for giving me the encouragement, love, and the space

Maryann Barber

CONTENTS

EXPLORING MICROSOFT® POWERPOINT® 2002

3

ANIMATING A PRESENTATION: PHOTOGRAPHS, DIAGRAMS, AND CHARTS   121

4

ADVANCED TECHNIQUES: SOUND, MASTERS, WEB PAGES, AND BROADCASTING   177

PREFACE

Continuing a tradition of excellence, Prentice Hall is proud to announce the latest update in Microsoft Office texts: the new Exploring Microsoft Office XP series by Robert T. Grauer and Maryann Barber.

The hands-on approach and conceptual framework of this comprehensive series helps students master all aspects of the Microsoft Office XP software, while providing the background necessary to transfer and use these skills in their personal and professional lives.

WHAT'S NEW IN THE EXPLORING OFFICE SERIES FOR XP

The entire Exploring Office series has been revised to include the new features found in the Office XP Suite, which contains Word 2002, Excel 2002, Access 2002, PowerPoint 2002, Publisher 2000, FrontPage 2002, and Outlook 2002.

In addition, this revision includes fully revised end of chapter material that provides an extensive review of concepts and techniques discussed in the chapter. Many of these exercises feature the World Wide Web and application integration.

Building on the success of the Web site provided for previous editions of this series, Exploring Office XP will introduce the MyPHLIP Companion Web site, a site customized for each instructor that includes on-line, interactive study guides, data file downloads, current news feeds, additional case studies and exercises, and other helpful information. Start out at www.prenhall.com/grauer to explore these resources!

Organization of the Exploring Office Series for XP

The new Exploring Microsoft Office XP series includes four combined Office XP texts from which to choose:

- *Volume I* is MOUS certified in each of the major applications in the Office suite (Word, Excel, Access, and PowerPoint). Three additional modules (Essential Computer Concepts, Essentials of Windows, and Essentials of the Internet) are also included.

- *Volume II* picks up where Volume I left off, covering the advanced topics for the individual applications. A VBA primer has been added.

- The ***Brief Microsoft Office XP*** edition provides less coverage of the individual applications than Volume I (a total of 8 chapters as opposed to 14). The supplementary modules (Windows, Internet, and Concepts) are not included.

- A new volume, ***Getting Started with Office XP***, contains the first chapter from each application (Word, Excel, Access, and PowerPoint), plus three additional modules: Essentials of Windows, Essentials of the Internet, and Essential Computer Concepts.

Individual texts for Word 2002, Excel 2002, Access 2002, and PowerPoint 2002 provide complete coverage of the application and are MOUS certified. For shorter courses, we have created brief versions of the Exploring texts that give students a four-chapter introduction to each application. Each of these volumes is MOUS certified at the Core level.

To complete the full coverage of this series, custom modules on Microsoft Outlook 2002, Microsoft FrontPage 2002, Microsoft Publisher 2002, and a generic introduction to Microsoft Windows are also available.

The Microsoft Office User Specialist (MOUS) program is globally recognized as the standard for demonstrating desktop skills with the Microsoft Office suite of business productivity applications (Microsoft Word, Microsoft Excel, Microsoft PowerPoint, Microsoft Access, and Microsoft Outlook). With a MOUS certification, thousands of people have demonstrated increased productivity and have proved their ability to utilize the advanced functionality of these Microsoft applications.

By encouraging individuals to develop advanced skills with Microsoft's leading business desktop software, the MOUS program helps fill the demand for qualified, knowledgeable people in the modern workplace. At the same time, MOUS helps satisfy an organization's need for a qualitative assessment of employee skills.

Customize the Exploring Office Series with Prentice Hall's Right PHit Binding Program

The Exploring Office XP series is part of the Right PHit Custom Binding Program, enabling instructors to create their own texts by selecting modules from Office XP Volume I, Volume II, Outlook, FrontPage, and Publisher to suit the needs of a specific course. An instructor could, for example, create a custom text consisting of the core modules in Word and Excel, coupled with the brief modules for Access and PowerPoint, and a brief introduction to computer concepts.

Instructors can also take advantage of Prentice Hall's Value Pack program to shrinkwrap multiple texts together at substantial savings to the student. A value pack is ideal in courses that require complete coverage of multiple applications.

The **Instructor's CD** that accompanies the Exploring Office series contains:

- Student data disks
- Solutions to all exercises and problems
- PowerPoint lectures
- Instructor's manuals in Word format enable the instructor to annotate portions of the instructor manual for distribution to the class
- A Windows-based test manager and the associated test bank in Word format

Prentice Hall's New MyPHLIP Companion Web site at www.prenhall.com/grauer offers current events, exercises, and downloadable supplements. This site also includes an on-line study guide containing true/false, multiple-choice, and essay questions.

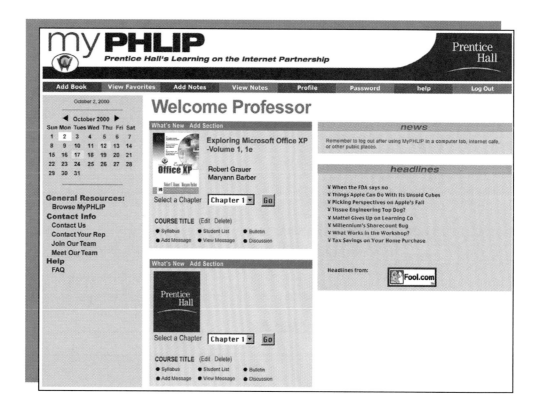

WebCT www.prenhall.com/webct

GOLD LEVEL CUSTOMER SUPPORT available exclusively to adopters of Prentice Hall courses is provided free-of-charge upon adoption and provides you with priority assistance, training discounts, and dedicated technical support.

Blackboard www.prenhall.com/blackboard

Prentice Hall's abundant on-line content, combined with Blackboard's popular tools and interface, result in robust Web-based courses that are easy to implement, manage, and use—taking your courses to new heights in student interaction and learning.

CourseCompass www.coursecompass.com

CourseCompass is a dynamic, interactive on-line course management tool powered by Blackboard. This exciting product allows you to teach with marketing-leading Pearson Education content in an easy-to-use customizable format.

Exploring Microsoft Office XP assumes no prior knowledge of the operating system. A 64-page section introduces the reader to the Essentials of Windows and provides an overview of the operating system. Students are shown the necessary file-management operations to use Microsoft Office successfully.

In-depth tutorials throughout all the Office XP applications enhance the conceptual introduction to each task and guide the student at the computer. Every step in every exercise has a full-color screen shot to illustrate the specific commands. Boxed tips provide alternative techniques and shortcuts and/or anticipate errors that students may make.

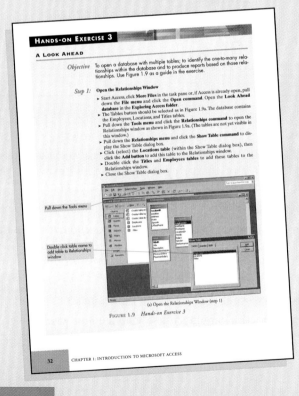

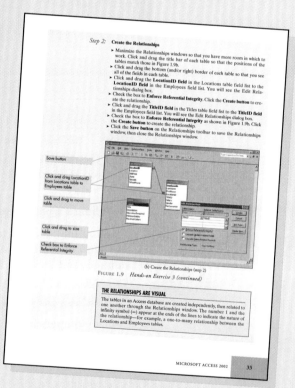

The authors have created an entirely new set of end-of-chapter exercises for every chapter in all of the applications. These new exercises have been written to provide the utmost in flexibility, variety, and difficulty.

Web-based Practice exercises and On Your Own exercises are marked by an icon in the margin and allow further exploration and practice via the World Wide Web.

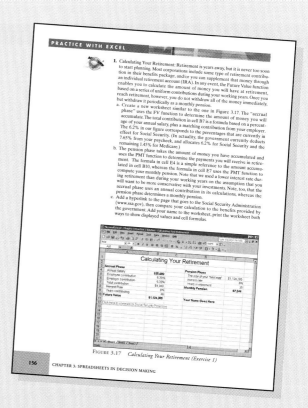

FIGURE 3.17   *Calculating Your Retirement (Exercise 1)*

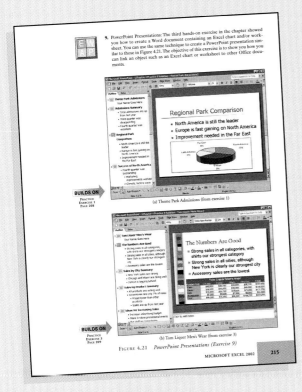

FIGURE 4.21   *PowerPoint Presentations (Exercise 9)*

Integration Exercises are marked by an icon in the margin. These exercises take advantage of the Microsoft Office Suite's power to use multiple applications in one document, spreadsheet, or presentation.

Builds On Exercises require students to use selected application files as the starting point in later exercises, thereby introducing new information to students only as needed.

The end-of-chapter material includes multiple-choice questions for self-evaluation plus additional "on your own" exercises to encourage the reader to further explore the application.

ACKNOWLEDGMENTS

We want to thank the many individuals who have helped to bring this project to fruition. Jodi McPherson, senior editor at Prentice Hall, has provided new leadership in extending the series to Office XP. Cathi Profitko did an absolutely incredible job on our Web site. Eileen Clark coordinated the myriad details of production and the certification process. Lynne Breitfeller was the project manager and manufacturing buyer. Greg Hubit has been masterful as the external production editor for every book in the series. Cecil Yarbrough did an outstanding job in checking the manuscript for technical accuracy. Chuck Cox did his usual fine work as copyeditor. Melissa Edwards was the supplements editor. Cindy Stevens, Tom McKenzie, and Michael Olmstead wrote the instructor manuals. Emily Knight and Sharon Turkovich coordinated the marketing. Patricia Smythe developed the innovative and attractive design. We also want to acknowledge our reviewers who, through their comments and constructive criticism, greatly improved the series.

Lynne Band, Middlesex Community College
Don Belle, Central Piedmont Community College
Stuart P. Brian, Holy Family College
Carl M. Briggs, Indiana University School of Business
Kimberly Chambers, Scottsdale Community College
Alok Charturvedi, Purdue University
Jerry Chin, Southwest Missouri State University
Dean Combellick, Scottsdale Community College
Cody Copeland, Johnson County Community College
Larry S. Corman, Fort Lewis College
Janis Cox, Tri-County Technical College
Martin Crossland, Southwest Missouri State University
Bill Daley, University of Oregon
Paul E. Daurelle, Western Piedmont Community College
Carolyn DiLeo, Westchester Community College
Judy Dolan, Palomar College
David Douglas, University of Arkansas
Carlotta Eaton, Radford University
Judith M. Fitspatrick, Gulf Coast Community College
James Franck, College of St. Scholastica
Raymond Frost, Central Connecticut State University
Midge Gerber, Southwestern Oklahoma State University
James Gips, Boston College
Vernon Griffin, Austin Community College
Ranette Halverson, Midwestern State University
Michael Hassett, Fort Hays State University
Mike Hearn, Community College of Philadelphia
Wanda D. Heller, Seminole Community College
Bonnie Homan, San Francisco State University
Ernie Ivey, Polk Community College
Mike Kelly, Community College of Rhode Island
Jane King, Everett Community College
Rose M. Laird, Northern Virginia Community College

David Langley, University of Oregon
John Lesson, University of Central Florida
Daniela Marghitu, Auburn University
David B. Meinert, Southwest Missouri State University
Alan Moltz, Naugatuck Valley Technical Community College
Kim Montney, Kellogg Community College
Bill Morse, DeVry Institute of Technology
Kevin Pauli, University of Nebraska
Mary McKenry Percival, University of Miami
Marguerite Nedreberg, Youngstown State University
Delores Pusins, Hillsborough Community College
Gale E. Rand, College Misericordia
Judith Rice, Santa Fe Community College
David Rinehard, Lansing Community College
Marilyn Salas, Scottsdale Community College
John Shepherd, Duquesne University
Barbara Sherman, Buffalo State College
Robert Spear, Prince George's Community College
Michael Stewardson, San Jacinto College—North
Helen Stoloff, Hudson Valley Community College
Margaret Thomas, Ohio University
Mike Thomas, Indiana University School of Business
Suzanne Tomlinson, Iowa State University
Karen Tracey, Central Connecticut State University
Antonio Vargas, El Paso Community College
Sally Visci, Lorain County Community College
David Weiner, University of San Francisco
Connie Wells, Georgia State University
Wallace John Whistance-Smith, Ryerson Polytechnic University
Jack Zeller, Kirkwood Community College

A final word of thanks to the unnamed students at the University of Miami, who make it all worthwhile. Most of all, thanks to you, our readers, for choosing this book. Please feel free to contact us with any comments and suggestions.

Robert T. Grauer
rgrauer@miami.edu
www.bus.miami.edu/~rgrauer
www.prenhall.com/grauer

Maryann Barber
mbarber@miami.edu
www.bus.miami.edu/~mbarber

Microsoft®

Exploring

PowerPoint® 2002

Chapters 3 and 4

CHAPTER 3

Animating a Presentation: Photographs, Diagrams, and Charts

OBJECTIVES

AFTER READING THIS CHAPTER YOU WILL BE ABLE TO:

1. Insert a photo album into a PowerPoint presentation; describe several variations in formatting that are possible within a photo album.
2. Describe the diagrams that are available within the Diagram Gallery; create a pyramid and a target diagram.
3. Create an organization chart; use the AutoFormat command and custom formatting to change the appearance of the default organization chart.
4. Use Microsoft Graph to create and edit a chart; distinguish between charts that plot the data series in rows and in columns.
5. Add custom animation to individual objects on a slide; change the order and/or duration in which the objects appear during a slide show.
6. Describe the different animation effects that are available; explain the color coding that is associated with different types of animation effects.
7. Animate an organization chart so that its shapes appear by level or branch.
8. Animate a graph so that the data appears by category or by series.

OVERVIEW

PowerPoint provides many different ways with which to animate a presentation. You can choose from a variety of entrance and/or exit effects, specify the sequence in which the objects appear on a slide, and control the timing of the individual effects. Moreover, the animation can be applied to any type of object—text, clip art, diagrams, or charts. This chapter describes how to use the special tools within Microsoft Office to create diagrams and charts, and then explains how to animate those objects to create dynamic presentations. We begin, however, by describing several ways in which to incorporate photographs into a presentation.

Figure 3.1 displays multiple slides from our first presentation, which illustrates how to work with photographs. The presentation is created from a series of pictures that are stored in their own folder from where they are inserted into the presentation. Each slide in Figure 3.1 illustrates a different capability.

The **photo album** in Figure 3.1a imports multiple photographs into a presentation, without having to format each picture individually. The photos may be taken from your hard disk, a scanner, or a digital camera. Regardless of the origin or file format of the photographs, you can specify how many pictures you want per slide (one, two, or four), choose from a variety of picture frames (rounded corners are used in our figure), and/or insert a caption below each picture.

Figure 3.1b displays cropped versions of two pictures in the original album. Compare these photographs to their counterparts in Figure 3.1a to see how we eliminated part of the background in order to focus on the happy couple. This was accomplished through the **Crop tool** on the **Picture toolbar**, which also contains additional tools to rotate a photograph and/or change the color or brightness. You can also compress a photograph (generally without a loss in quality) within a presentation to reduce the file size.

Figure 3.1c illustrates one of our favorite techniques, which is to use a photograph as a fill effect for the background of the slide. The slide itself is "empty"; it does not contain a photograph or even a title (although a title could be added to describe the photograph). Instead, the **Format Background command** was used to select the photograph as a background for the slide, in effect, creating a presentation that bears no resemblance to a typical PowerPoint presentation.

Figure 3.1d applies a custom animation effect to dissolve a black and white photograph into its color counterpart. The original color photograph is duplicated and saved as a black and white photograph, with the latter placed directly on top. An exit effect (dissolve out) is applied to the black and white picture, thus creating the transition. It's a simple and effective technique that adds variety to a presentation.

Figure 3.1e combines WordArt with a picture background. WordArt was used to create the initial object (the word "love") after which the **Format WordArt command** was used to apply the photograph as fill. The only tricky part (if any) is to choose the photograph and text in such a way as to not obscure an essential portion of the underlying picture. The crop tool may be useful, therefore, to alter a picture prior to selecting it as fill.

Figure 3.1f uses animation in conjunction with a sound file to create a musical ending in which the photographs scroll continuously on the slide while the music plays in the background. The four original photographs are arranged one on top of another, extending above and below the slide. All four photographs are selected, and the custom animation command is applied. The sound (music) file is inserted independently and timed to play simultaneously with the scrolling of the pictures.

Photographs, File Formats, and File Folders

A photograph may be stored anywhere on a hard disk, although beginners typically store all photographs in the **My Pictures folder** within their My Documents folder. You may create additional folders (within the My Pictures folder and/or anywhere on your system) to hold groups of pictures. You can move and copy photographs from one folder to another, or from one device to another, such as from a hard disk to a zip drive, floppy disk, or CD (provided you have the software to write to the CD).

A photograph has the same attributes as any other file, which include the file name, type, file size, and date the file was created or last modified. There are many different file types for graphic work. The **Joint Photographic Experts Group** (**JPG**, pronounced "jpeg") format is the most common for photographs. The **Graphics Interchange Format** (**GIF**, pronounced "jif") is used for clip art and similar images.

(a) Photo Album

(b) Revised (cropped) Photos

(c) Photo as Background

(d) Black and White Transition

(e) WordArt

(f) Credits and Sound

FIGURE 3.1   *Fun with Photographs*

Transitions and Animations

Transitions and animations are similar in that both add interest to a presentation through movement and (optionally) sound. A *transition* applies to the slide as a whole and controls the way the entire slide moves on and off the screen. An *animation* controls the appearance of individual elements on a single slide. PowerPoint includes a selection of animation schemes that can be applied to selected slides and/or to the presentation as a whole. PowerPoint also gives you the ability to create a *custom animation*, which requires that you determine when (in what sequence) the objects appear and how the objects make their entrance (e.g., whether they fly in from the top or bottom). You can also control how long the objects are to remain on the screen and if (how) they are to exit. The objects on a slide may include text boxes, clip art, photographs, and so on.

Each slide in Figure 3.2 has its own entrance and exit effect, denoted by a green and red icon, respectively. (The effects from which you can choose are divided into subtle, moderate, and exciting, and it is fun to experiment.) The sequence and duration of the individual animations are seen in the associated timeline. The entrance of the Los Angeles photo is triggered by clicking the mouse during the slide show. This is followed automatically by the exit of this object, followed by the entrance of the next photo, followed by the exit of the photo. Each effect takes two seconds (medium speed) as indicated on the timeline. Most animation options include an optional sound effect; for example, you can specify the sound of a clicking camera as each photograph makes its appearance.

Any animated slide can be thought of as a theatrical production unto itself. The objects on a PowerPoint slide, just like the actors in a Broadway show, must be thoroughly scripted so that the performance is as effective as possible. You can select multiple objects at the same time in order to apply the same effects in a single command. You can resequence an animation by clicking the re-order arrows up or down within the custom animation task pane. You can change and/or remove effects as necessary. It's fun, it's easy, and as you may have guessed, it's time for our first hands-on exercise.

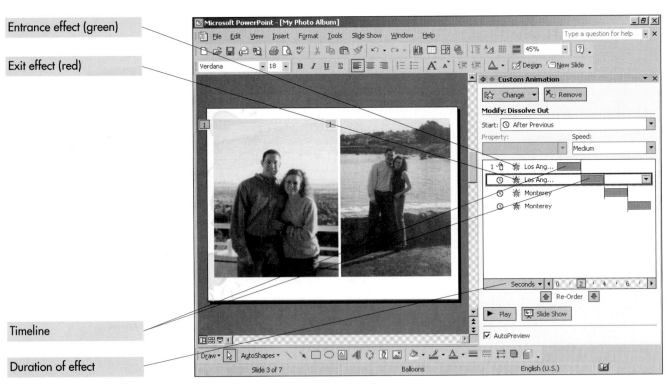

FIGURE 3.2 *The Basics of Custom Animation*

FUN WITH PHOTOGRAPHS

Objective   Create a photo album; use cropping and other techniques to enhance individual photographs, apply custom animation to various slides.

Step 1:   **Create a Photo Album**

> ➤ Start PowerPoint. Close any open presentations. Pull down the **Insert menu**, click **Picture**, then click **New Photo Album** to display the Photo Album dialog box.
> ➤ Click the **File/Disk command button** to select from existing photos on your computer. You can use your own photos or you can use our pictures, which are in the **Our Photos folder** within the **Exploring PowerPoint folder**.
> ➤ Press and hold the **Ctrl key** as you select the four pictures in Figure 3.3a. (Be sure to include **Los Angeles** and **Monterey** as we will crop these photos in a later step.) Click the **Insert button**.

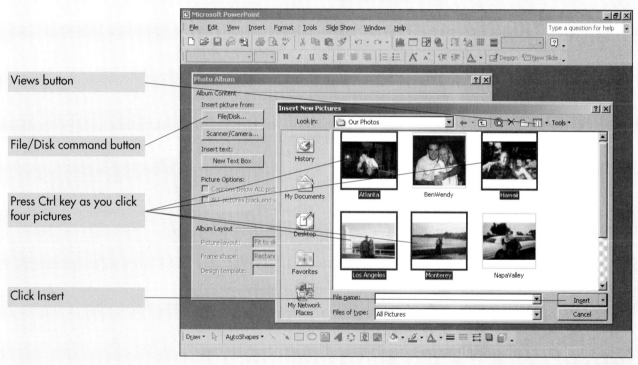

(a) Create a Photo Album (step 1)

FIGURE 3.3   *Hands-on Exercise 1*

CHANGE THE VIEW

Use the Views button to cycle through the different views that are available with photographs. The Thumbnails view is ideal for selecting a picture as it displays a miniature version of the photograph. The Details view provides the most information, and further, it enables you to sequence your files according to any attribute. Click the Size column, for example, and you arrange the pictures according to file size. Click the column a second time to switch from ascending to descending sequence and vice versa.

Step 2:   **Choose the Album Layout**

➤ You should see the Photo Album dialog box as shown in Figure 3.3b. You can change the order of the photos within the album by selecting a photo, then pressing the **up** or **down arrow** as necessary.

➤ Look toward the bottom of the dialog box (in the Album Layout area) and make the indicated selections. We chose **4 pictures** for the layout and **Rounded Rectangle** for the Frame shape.

➤ Click the **Browse button**, select a design template (we chose **Balloons**), then click **Select** to close the dialog box. Click the **Create button** to create the album and close the Photo Album dialog box.

➤ You should see a presentation consisting of two slides. The first slide is the title slide and is created automatically. The second slide contains the four pictures you selected.

➤ If your layout is different from ours, pull down the **Format menu**, click the **Photo Album command** to display the associated dialog box, and enter the correct parameters. Click the **Update button**.

➤ If necessary, change the title slide to include your name. Save the presentation as **My Photo Album**.

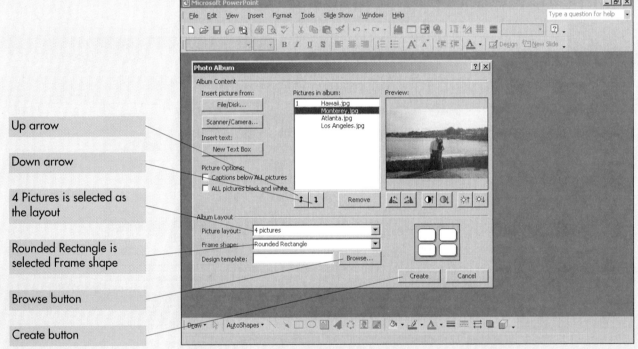

(b) Choose the Album Layout (step 2)

FIGURE 3.3   *Hands-on Exercise 1 (continued)*

TOUCH UP YOUR PHOTOS

It's not PhotoShop, but the Format Photo Album command provides limited capability to modify a photograph. Select the appropriate picture within the Format Photo Album dialog box, then use the appropriate tool on the Picture toolbar. You can rotate a picture left or right, increase or decrease the contrast, and/or increase or decrease the brightness. You can also point to any tool to display a ScreenTip that is indicative of its function.

Step 3: **Add Custom Animation**

> ➤ Change to the **Normal view** if necessary. Click the **Slides tab** in the left pane so that you see a slide miniature of every slide in the presentation. Pull down the **Slide Show menu** and click **Custom Animation** to open the task pane as shown in Figure 3.3c.
> ➤ Select the second slide. Press and hold the **Ctrl key** as you select all four photos. Click the **Add Effect button**, click **Entrance**, then select **Dissolve In** for the effect. (Click the **More Effects subcommand** if you do not see the Dissolve In effect.) Click the **down arrow** in the **Speed list box** and select **Slow**.
> ➤ Click a **down arrow** next to any effect and click **Start After Previous** so that the pictures are displayed one after another, without having to click the mouse.
> ➤ Be sure that all four animation effects are still selected, then click a **down arrow** next to any effect, and click **Effect Options** to display the Dissolve In dialog box. Click the **Effect tab**, click the **down arrow** for the **Sound list box** and (scroll if necessary to) choose **Camera**.
> ➤ Click **OK** to accept the sound and close the dialog box. Save the presentation.

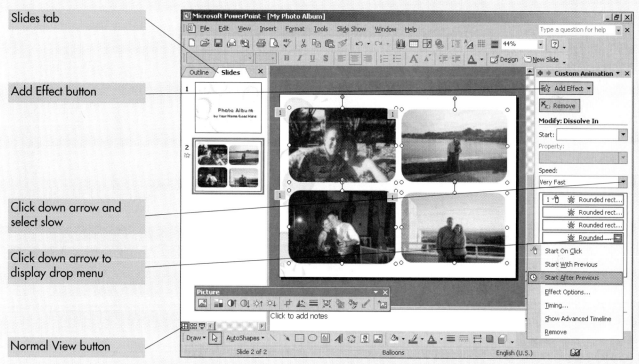

(c) Add Custom Animation (step 3)

FIGURE 3.3   *Hands-on Exercise 1 (continued)*

COMPRESS YOUR PICTURES

Use the Compress Pictures command to (attempt to) reduce the size of a presentation. Save the presentation before you begin because the command cannot be undone. Select any picture, then click the Compress Pictures tool on the Picture toolbar to display the associated dialog box. Check the options to compress pictures and to delete the cropped areas of pictures. Click OK, then click the Apply button when warned that you might reduce the quality of the photographs. Review the presentation. If the quality is significantly less (it rarely is), exit the presentation without saving to return to the original.

Step 4: **Crop a Picture**

➤ Click the **New Slide button** to insert a new slide. Change the slide layout to a blank slide. Close the task pane.

➤ Pull down the **Insert menu**, click **Picture**, click **From File**, then select the **Monterey picture** from the **Our Photos folder** in the **Exploring PowerPoint folder**. Click **Insert**.

➤ Insert the **LA picture** in similar fashion. (You must insert the original pictures; you cannot copy the photographs from slide two because the Photo Album command disables cropping.)

➤ Select the LA photo as shown in the figure. The picture toolbar should be visible, but if not, pull down the **View menu**, **click Toolbars**, then click the **Picture toolbar**. Use the **cropping tool** to crop the picture as shown in Figure 3.3d.

➤ Once you are satisfied with the result, click off the picture, then click and drag a corner to resize (enlarge) the cropped image. Crop the Monterey photo in similar fashion. Add animation as you see fit.

➤ Try to size the resulting photos identically for symmetry on this slide. Save the presentation.

(d) Crop a Picture (step 4)

FIGURE 3.3   *Hands-on Exercise 1 (continued)*

SAVE THE NEW PICTURE

Once you have modified a picture, by cropping, shading, or any other technique, you can save the new picture as a replacement for the original. Right click the photo to display a context-sensitive menu. Choose the Save as Picture command, specify JPEG or GIF as the file format, then choose the folder where you want to save the photo. Click the Save button. You can now use the modified picture in all subsequent photo albums.

Step 5: **Set a Picture as the Background**

> ➤ Our favorite technique is to create presentations that do not look as though they were created in PowerPoint. One way to accomplish this is to create a blank slide that contains nothing other than a single photograph as the slide background.
> ➤ Insert a blank slide at the end of the presentation. Pull down the **Format command** and click the **Background** command to display the Background dialog box in Figure 3.3e.
> ➤ Click the **down arrow** in the **Background Fill** area, click **Fill Effects** to display the associated dialog box, then click the **Picture tab**.
> ➤ Click the **Select Picture command button**, then select the desired photo (e.g., **BenWendy** in the **Our Photos folder**).
> ➤ Click **Insert** to select the picture, click **OK**, then click the **Apply button** to set the photograph as the background for this slide.
> ➤ It's easy and effective. The only "trick" is to choose a photo that has the approximate proportions of the slide.
> ➤ Save the presentation.

(e) Set a Picture as the Background (step 5)

FIGURE 3.3 *Hands-on Exercise 1 (continued)*

PRINTING THE PRESENTATION

We're not sure why, but the slide background may not print on a black and white printer. If this is true on your configuration (click the Print Preview button to find out), pull down the File menu, click the Print command, then choose Color in the Color/Grayscale list box even if you have a black and white printer.

Step 6: **From Black and White to Color**

➤ Insert a blank slide at the end of the presentation. Pull down the **Insert menu**, click **Picture**, click **From File**, then select the **BenWendy picture** from the **Our Photos folder**. Click **Insert**.

➤ Ben and Wendy should appear on a blank slide, with the picture selected. Size the picture, press **Ctrl+C** to copy it, then press **Ctrl+V** to duplicate it.

➤ Right click the top picture, then click the **Format Picture command** to display the associated dialog box. Click the **Picture tab**, then click the **down arrow** on the **Color list box** in the Image control area. Select **Black and White** and click **OK**.

➤ Check that the top picture is still selected, pull down the **Slide Show menu**, and click **Custom Animation** to open the task pane as shown in Figure 3.3f. Click the **Add Effect button**, click **Exit**, then click **Dissolve Out**. Change the speed to **Very slow**. Close the task pane.

➤ Click and drag the black and white photo so that it is directly on top of the color photo (see the boxed tip for additional hints). Click the **Slide Show button** to see the finished slide, then click the black and white photograph to dissolve to color. Press **Esc**.

(f) From Black and White to Color (step 6)

FIGURE 3.3 *Hands-on Exercise 1 (continued)*

PLACE ONE PHOTO ON TOP OF ANOTHER

Press and hold the Ctrl key to select both pictures, pull down the Format menu, and click Picture to display the Format Picture dialog box. Click the Size tab, then enter the appropriate dimensions (e.g., a width of 7 inches for Ben and Wendy). Check the box to lock the aspect ratio so as not to distort the picture. Click the Position tab and enter horizontal and vertical distances from the left corner. Click OK. Both photos are still selected, and you can click and drag to "fine tune" the size and position.

Step 7: **Create the WordArt**

> ➤ Insert a blank slide at the end of the presentation. Click the **Insert WordArt button** on the Drawing toolbar to display the WordArt Gallery dialog box. Choose any style you like (we took the first style in the first row). Click **OK**.
> ➤ You should see the Edit WordArt Text box. Enter **LOVE** (in uppercase) as the text for your WordArt object. Click **OK** to insert the WordArt into your presentation. Move and size the WordArt object so that it takes the entire slide as shown in Figure 3.3g.
> ➤ Pull down the **Format menu** and click **WordArt** to display the Format WordArt dialog box. Click the **Colors and Lines tab**, click the **down arrow** in the **Color list box** (in the Fill section), and select **Fill Effects** to display the Fill Effects dialog box.
> ➤ Click the **Picture tab**. Click the **Select Picture button**. Select the **BenWendy photo** and click **Insert**. Click **OK** to close the Fill Effects dialog box. Click **OK** a second time to close the Format WordArt dialog box.
> ➤ You should see the completed WordArt object with the photo as the fill for the letters. (You may have to resize the WordArt and/or use a cropped photo to better position the photo inside the text.) Save the presentation.

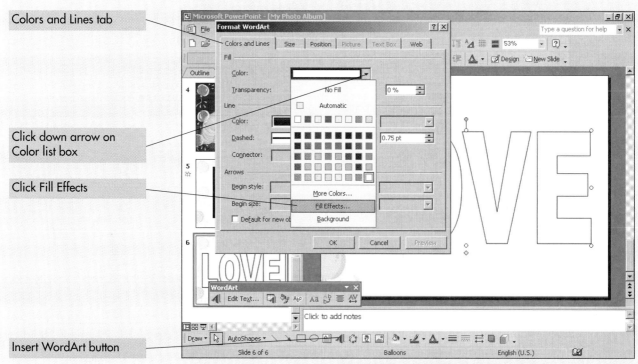

Colors and Lines tab

Click down arrow on Color list box

Click Fill Effects

Insert WordArt button

(g) Create the WordArt (step 7)

FIGURE 3.3 *Hands-on Exercise 1 (continued)*

THE WORDART TOOLBAR

The WordArt toolbar provides the easiest way to change an existing WordArt object. It is displayed automatically when a WordArt object is selected (and suppressed otherwise). As with any toolbar, you can point to a button to display a ScreenTip containing the name of the button, which is indicative of its function. You will find buttons to display the text vertically, change the style or shape, and/or edit the text.

Step 8:   **Create the Credits Slide**

➤ Press **Ctrl+Home** to move to the beginning of the presentation. Select (click) the second slide, which is the original "photo album" that contains the four photographs. Press **Ctrl+C** to copy the slide.

➤ Press **Ctrl+End** to move to the end of the presentation. Press **Ctrl+V** to paste the slide at the end of the presentation.

➤ Arrange the photographs in a filmstrip. The end result will have a picture above and below the actual slide as shown in Figure 3.3h. Give yourself additional room in which to work by changing the zoom percentage and/or making the notes pane smaller.

➤ Pull down the **Slide Show menu** and click **Custom Animation**. Delete all of the existing animation effects. (The existing effects are the transition to the sound of a camera that we added at the beginning of the presentation.)

➤ Press and hold the **Ctrl key** to select all four pictures. Click the **Add Effect button**, click **Entrance**, click **More Effects**, scroll to the **Exciting category**, then choose **Credits**.

➤ You should see a preview of the effect in which the pictures scroll onto the screen just as in a list of movie credits. Click **OK**. Save the presentation.

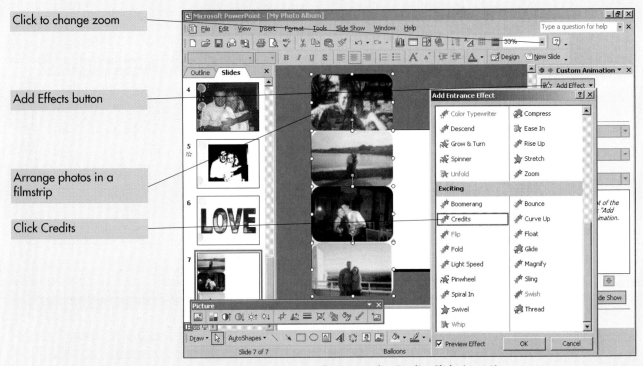

Click to change zoom

Add Effects button

Arrange photos in a filmstrip

Click Credits

(h) Create the Credits Slide (step 8)

FIGURE 3.3   *Hands-on Exercise 1 (continued)*

USE THE GRID FOR EASY ALIGNMENT

Pull down the View menu, click the Grid and Guides command to display the associated dialog box, then check the boxes to snap objects to the grid and to display the grid on screen. The grid is visible when you work in PowerPoint, but it does not appear during a slide show or on the printed version of a presentation. Use the grid to align objects more precisely on a slide, especially in relation to one another.

Step 9:   **Add the Sound and Animation**

> Pull down the **Insert menu**, click **Movies and Sounds**, then choose **Sound from File** to display the Insert Sound dialog box. Change to the **Our Photos folder**, specify **All Files** as the file type, then insert **Beethoven's Symphony 9**. Click **OK**.

> Click **Yes** when asked whether you want the sound to play automatically. Click and drag the animation for Beethoven's symphony to the top of the Custom animation list as shown in Figure 3.3i. (The zero next to the effect indicates that the sound will play automatically.)

> Click the animation for the first rounded rectangle (photograph), then press and hold the **Ctrl key** as you select the transition effects for the other photographs. Click the **down arrow** next to the last rectangle, then click **Start with Previous**.

> Click the **down arrow** next to the last effect, click **Timing** to display the Credits list box, then set the repeat list box **Until Next Click** so that the pictures scroll continually. Move the pictures to the middle of the slide.

> Turn up the sound on your computer, then click the **Play button**. Close the task pane. Click and drag the **Sound icon** to the lower-right portion of the slide.

> Save the presentation.

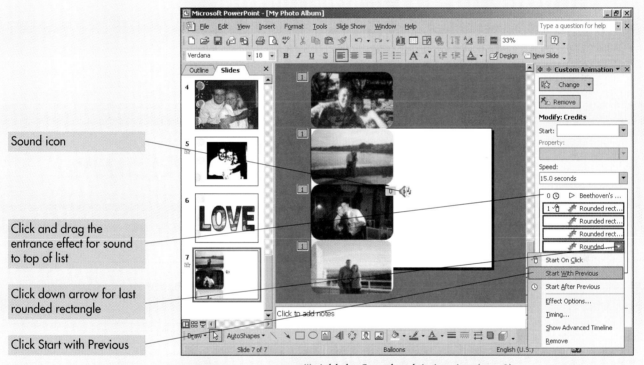

Sound icon

Click and drag the entrance effect for sound to top of list

Click down arrow for last rounded rectangle

Click Start with Previous

(i) Add the Sound and Animation (step 9)

FIGURE 3.3   *Hands-on Exercise 1 (continued)*

FIND THE MUSIC

Windows XP ships with multiple sound files to illustrate various features in the operating system. The trick is to find the music. Click the Start button on the Windows taskbar, click Search to display the Search Results dialog box, then click Pictures, Music, or Video. Check the box for music, click the Search button, and then wait as Windows searches for all of the music files on your system. Right click any sound file, then click the Play command to listen to the music.

Step 10:   **Show Time**

➤ Press **Ctrl+Home** to move to the first slide. Print the presentation in the form of audience handouts for your instructor. Save the presentation a final time.

➤ Click the **Slide Show button** (at the bottom of the window) to show the presentation as shown in Figure 3.3j. Think about the various techniques that were used to create the slides:

- Slide 2 (the four photographs) was created initially as a photo album. The animation effects (the click of the camera) were added manually.
- Slide 3 contains two photos that were cropped for better composition.
- Slide 4 displays a photo as the background for a slide.
- Slide 5 uses a transition effect to colorize a black and white photograph.
- Slide 6 uses a photograph as the background for a WordArt object.
- Slide 7 uses sound and the credits animation effect.

➤ Press **Esc** to end the presentation. Exit PowerPoint if you do not want to continue with the next exercise at this time.

(j) Show Time (step 10)

FIGURE 3.3   *Hands-on Exercise 1 (continued)*

USE YOUR PICTURES AS A SCREEN SAVER

Right click the desktop to display a context-sensitive menu, click Properties to display the Properties dialog box, click the Screen Saver tab, and choose My Picture Slide Slideshow. Click the Settings tab, click the Browse button, and select the folder containing your photographs. We suggest that you change the picture every seven seconds, that the pictures take the entire screen, and that you use transition effects between pictures. Click OK to accept the settings you have chosen, then click the Preview button to view the screen saver. (This tip works in Windows XP and may not work in previous versions.)

Figure 3.4 displays a six-slide presentation for a hypothetical "Super Zoo." The presentation is interesting in and of itself; what you cannot see, however, is the animation that is associated with every slide. The giraffe in slide one, for example, is made to walk across the slide, and then disappear. The boxes in the organization chart on slide two appear one branch at a time, as do the columns in the chart on slide three. There are "exploding fireworks" on the last slide.

The presentation also includes additional objects that we have not seen previously. The organization chart in slide two is created through the Diagram Gallery (as described below). The chart in slide three is created through Microsoft Graph, a charting program that is built into Microsoft Office. (Charts can also be imported from Microsoft Excel.)

The timeline in slide four is developed from a table. Look closely, and you should see the structure of an underlying 2 x 12 table (two rows and 12 columns, the latter corresponding to the months of the year). Clip art and block arrows were placed on top of the table to create the timeline. Animation was added at the end, so that the arrows (milestones in the project) appear sequentially.

The drawing in slide five was created using various tools on the Drawing toolbar. Clip art was placed on top of the various shapes, after which animation was applied to the individual objects. Slide six uses the AutoShapes tool to create an exploding slide in conjunction with sound and animation.

As indicated, animation is the common element in every slide and the driving concept throughout this chapter. Before we can apply the animation, however, we must first describe how to create the various objects on the slides. We begin with the organization chart on slide two.

The Diagram Gallery

An organization chart is one of six types of diagrams that can be created using the *Diagram Gallery* in Microsoft Office. Each diagram is intended to convey a different type of relationship that may exist within an organization. We focus on the organization chart, but it is useful to mention all six diagram types. Thus, we use

- *Organization Chart* to show hierarchical relationships
- *Cycle diagram* to show a process with a continuous cycle
- *Radial diagram* to show elements revolving around a core
- *Pyramid diagram* to show foundation relationships
- *Venn diagram* to show overlap between elements
- *Target diagram* to show steps toward a goal

All diagrams are developed within the *drawing canvas* (an area enclosed within hashed lines) that appears when you first create the diagram. Every diagram has a default format, which contains a limited number of entries (shapes). You can insert additional shapes such as subordinate or coworker boxes on an organization chart. You can also delete existing shapes (e.g., a specific box on an organization chart) by selecting the box and pressing the Del key.

You can change the appearance of a diagram as well as its structure. All diagrams provide access to the *AutoFormat tool* that displays a Style Gallery, which formats the diagram as a whole. Alternatively, you can select individual (and/or multiple) shapes within a diagram and format them independently. You can change the style of the connecting lines in an organization chart as well as their color. You can also change the font and/or alignment of the text within the individual shapes. It's easy, it's fun, and as you might have guessed, it is time for our next hands-on exercise.

(a) Title Slide

(b) Organization Chart

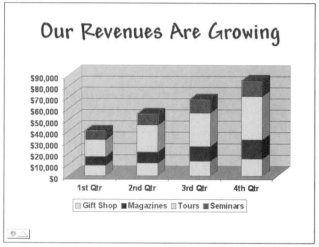

(c) Chart

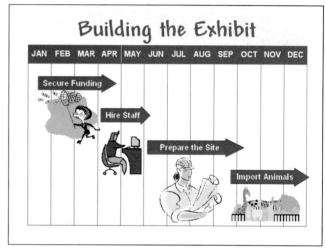

(d) Timeline (table)

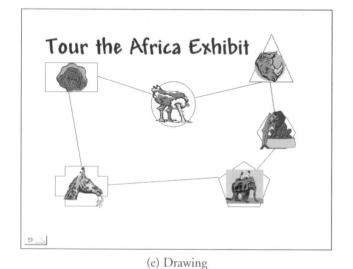

(e) Drawing

(f) AutoShape

FIGURE 3.4 *The Super Zoo Presentation*

DIAGRAMS AND ORGANIZATION CHARTS

Objective To create and format an organization chart; to create a pyramid and target using the Diagram Gallery. Use Figure 3.5 as a guide in the exercise.

Step 1: **Insert a Diagram**

➤ Start PowerPoint. Click the **New button** to begin a new presentation. Enter the title **Diagrams and Organization Charts** and your name on the title slide.

➤ Save the presentation as **Diagrams and Organization Charts** in the **Exploring PowerPoint folder**.

➤ Click the **New Slide button** to insert a new slide. If necessary, click the **down arrow** at the top of the task pane and select **Slide Layout**. Scroll in the task pane until you can select (click) the **Title and Diagram or Organization Chart layout**.

➤ Double click the icon to **add diagram or organization chart** to display the Diagram Gallery as shown in Figure 3.5a. Select **Organization Chart**. Click **OK**.

➤ Your slide should contain the default organization chart surrounded by a non-printing hashed line to indicate the drawing area. Close the task pane.

New button

New Slide button

Click Organization Chart

Title and Diagram or
Organization Chart layout

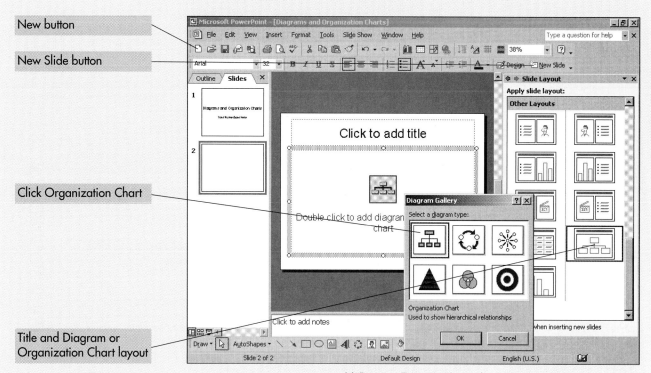

(a) Insert a Diagram (step 1)

FIGURE 3.5 *Hands-on Exercise 2*

USE THE TOOLBAR BUTTONS

You don't have to change the slide layout to insert a diagram onto an existing slide. Just select the slide, and then click the Insert Diagram or Organization button on the Drawing toolbar. The Drawing toolbar also contains buttons to insert WordArt or clip art.

Step 2:   **Create the Organization Chart**

➤ Click the **title place holder** and enter the title of this slide, **The Organization of Our Zoo**, as shown in Figure 3.5b.

➤ Click in the top box of the organization chart and type **Super Zoo**. (Do not press the enter key or you will create an extra line and unnecessarily increase the depth of the box.)

➤ Click in the **leftmost box** on the second line and type **Asian Exhibit**. Stay in the box after you have entered the text, click the **down arrow** on the **Insert Shape tool** in the Organization toolbar, and click **Subordinate**.

➤ Click in the newly created box (which appears under the Asian Exhibit) and type **Bengal Tigers** as shown in Figure 3.5b.

➤ Add **Komodo Dragons** as a second subordinate for **Asian Exhibit**. Enter the text for the remaining boxes as shown in Figure 3.5b. (The remaining boxes in the second row are **Aviary** and **Australian Exhibit**. **Kangaroos** and **Koala Bears** are subordinates for the **Australian Exhibit**.)

➤ Save the presentation.

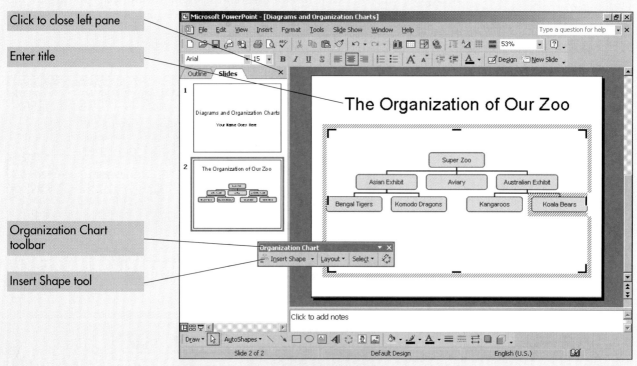

(b) Create the Organization Chart (step 2)

FIGURE 3.5   *Hands-on Exercise 2 (continued)*

IF YOU MAKE A MISTAKE

You can delete any box in the organization chart by selecting the box and pressing the Del key. If necessary, you can delete the entire chart (and start over) by clicking the hashed line surrounding the drawing area and pressing the Del key. You can also cancel (reverse) the last command(s) by clicking the Undo button or using the Ctrl+Z keyboard shortcut.

Step 3: **Add the African Exhibit**

➤ Close the left pane to give yourself additional room in which to work. (You can reopen the left pane at any time by clicking the **Normal View button** above the status bar.)

➤ Add the **African Exhibit** in one of two ways:
  • Click at the top of the organization chart and insert a **subordinate**, *or*
  • Click in the rightmost box on the second level and insert a **coworker**.

➤ Type **African Exhibit** in the box that appears at the end of the second line. Enter **Giraffes** and **Elephants** as subordinates for this box. Do not be concerned that the organization chart is becoming awkward due to its increased width.

➤ Click the **African Exhibit box**, click **Layout** on the Organization Chart toolbar to display the available layouts as shown in Figure 3.5c, and select **Right Hanging**. The subordinate boxes appear one under the other, as opposed to horizontally.

➤ Add **Lions** and **Tigers** as additional subordinates to the African Exhibit. Save the presentation.

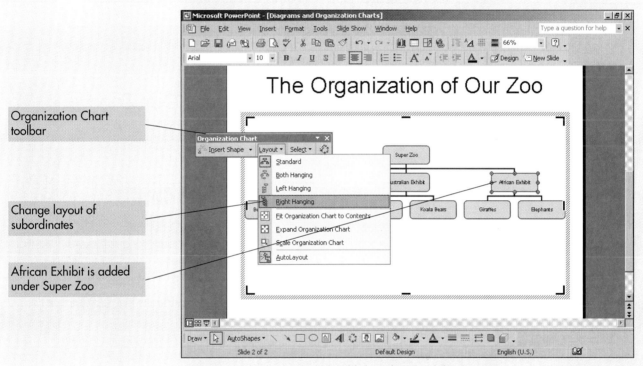

(c) Add the African Exhibit (step 3)

FIGURE 3.5 *Hands-on Exercise 2 (continued)*

THE ORGANIZATION CHART TOOLBAR

The Organization Chart toolbar appears automatically when the chart is selected and disappears when the chart is no longer active. The Insert Shape tool adds a subordinate (a box on the level below the selected box), a coworker (a box on the same level as the selected box), or an Assistant (a staff position). The Layout tool changes the design of the chart, the size of the drawing area, or the size of chart within the drawing area. Experiment with the different options. Use the Undo command if the results are unexpected or different from what you intended.

Step 4:   **Format the Chart**

➤ Right click any box in the organization chart to display a context-sensitive menu, and, if necessary, toggle the **Use AutoFormat command** off (the check should disappear).

➤ Click the **Super Zoo box** at the top of the organization chart. Click the **down arrow** next to the **Select tool** in the Organization toolbar and click **Branch** to select the entire organization chart.

➤ Pull down the **Format menu**. Click **AutoShape** to display the associated dialog box. Click the **Colors and Lines tab**, then click the **down arrow** next to the **color box** (in the fill area) and select **red**. Click **OK**.

➤ Click off the chart, click the **African Exhibit box**, click the **down arrow** next to the **Select tool** and click **Branch**. Use the **Format AutoShape command** to change the color of this branch to blue.

➤ Reselect all of the boxes in the organization chart. Click the **Font Size list box** on the Formatting toolbar and enter **11-point** type. Click the **Bold button** to change the font to bold. Click the **down arrow** next to the **Font color box** on the Formatting toolbar. Click **White**. Save the presentation.

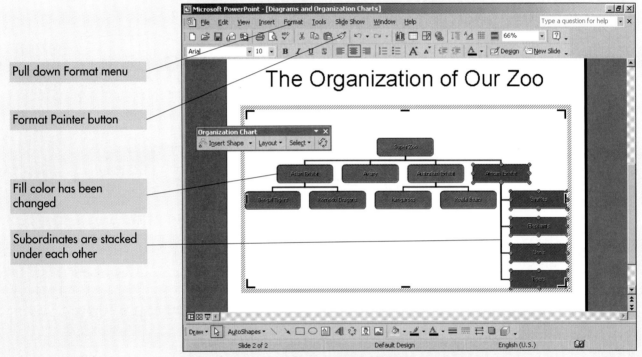

Pull down Format menu

Format Painter button

Fill color has been changed

Subordinates are stacked under each other

(d) Format the Chart (step 4)

FIGURE 3.5   *Hands-on Exercise 2 (continued)*

THE FORMAT PAINTER

The Format Painter copies the formatting of the selected text to other places in a presentation. Select the text with the formatting you want to copy, then click or double click the Format Painter. Clicking the button will paint only one selection. Double clicking the button will paint multiple selections until the feature is turned off by again clicking the button. Either way, the mouse pointer changes to a paintbrush, which you can drag over text to give it the formatting characteristics of the original selection.

Step 5: **Create a Pyramid Diagram**

➤ Click the **Normal View button** above the status bar and then click the **Slides tab** to check your progress. You should see the newly created organization chart as the second slide in your presentation.
➤ Click the **New Slide button**, then scroll in the Slide Layout task pane until you can select (click) the **Title and Diagram or Organization Chart layout**. Close the task pane.
➤ Double click the icon to **add diagram or organization chart** to display the Diagram Gallery. Click the **Pyramid Diagram icon**. Click **OK**. The default pyramid is created with three components.
➤ Click (select) the top triangle. Click the **Insert Shape button** on the Diagram toolbar twice in a row so that the pyramid has five components. Enter the text of each component as shown in Figure 3.5e.
➤ Click the **AutoFormat button** on the Diagram toolbar to display the Diagram Style Gallery. Select (click) the **Primary Colors** design, then click the **Apply button** to implement this design. Each block on the pyramid is now a different color.
➤ Click in the title place holder and enter **Sponsorship Levels** as the title of the slide. Save the presentation.

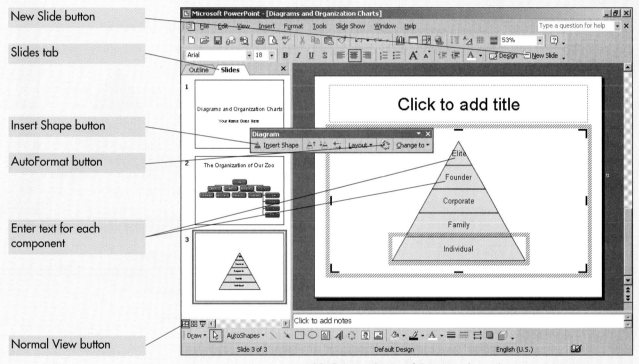

(e) Create a Pyramid Diagram (step 5)

FIGURE 3.5 *Hands-on Exercise 2 (continued)*

AUTOFORMAT ON AND OFF

You can format individual elements within a diagram provided that auto formatting is not in effect. Right click any element (e.g., a shape in a pyramid or a box in a hierarchy chart), toggle the Use AutoFormat command off (the check should disappear), then use the Format AutoShape command to display the associated dialog box. Click the Colors and Lines tab, change the fill color, line color, and/or thickness as desired, then click OK.

Step 6: **Create a Target Diagram**

➤ Select (click) any element on the pyramid. Click the **Layout button** on the Diagram toolbar, then click **Fit Diagram to Contents**.
➤ The size of the drawing canvas shrinks to more closely surround the pyramid. Click and drag the canvas to the left side of the slide.
➤ Click the **Copy button** on the Standard toolbar (or use the **Ctrl+C** keyboard shortcut). Click the **Paste button** (or press **Ctrl+V**). You should now have two pyramids side by side as shown in Figure 3.5f.
➤ Select the second pyramid, click the **Change to button** on the Diagram toolbar, and select **Target** to change the second pyramid to a target.
➤ Move and size the two diagrams as necessary, so that they both fit comfortably on the slide.
➤ Save the presentation.

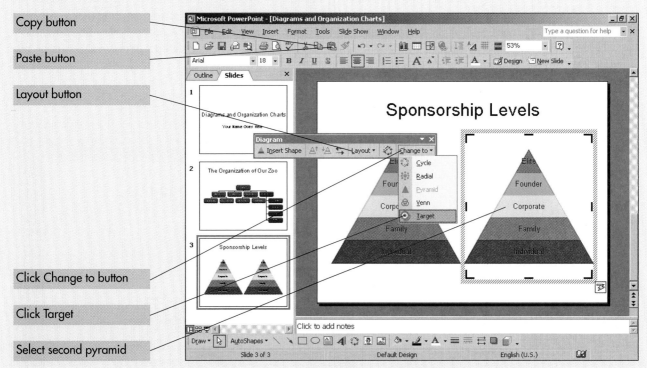

(f) Create a Target Diagram (step 6)

FIGURE 3.5 *Hands-on Exercise 2 (continued)*

THE DIAGRAM TOOLBAR

Start with one of five diagram types (radial, cycle, pyramid, Venn, or target), then click the Change to button to convert to a different type, while retaining all of your text and formatting information. Each diagram type has a unique strength and you can experiment to find the best diagram type to deliver your message. (Organization charts have their own toolbar and are not convertible to another diagram type.) Use the Insert Shape button to add the appropriate shape to any diagram. You can also use the AutoFormat button to display the Diagram Style Gallery to format the diagram as a whole.

Step 7: **Print the Audience Handouts**

➤ Pull down the **File menu** and click the **Print command** to display the Print dialog box. Click the **down arrow** in the **Print What** area and select **Handouts**. Specify **three slides** per page. Check the box to **frame the slides**.

➤ Click the **Preview button** to display a screen similar to Figure 3.5g. The complete presentation consists of three slides. The target diagram is on the last slide. A series of ruled lines appears next to each slide.

➤ Click the **Options button**, then click the **Header and Footer command** to display the associated dialog box. Check the box to include **Date and time**, then choose the option to **Update automatically**.

➤ Enter **your name and class** as the header. Click the **Apply to All button**, then click the **Print button** and click **OK** to print the audience handouts for your instructor. Close the Preview window.

➤ Save the presentation a final time. Exit PowerPoint if you do not want to continue with the next exercise at this time.

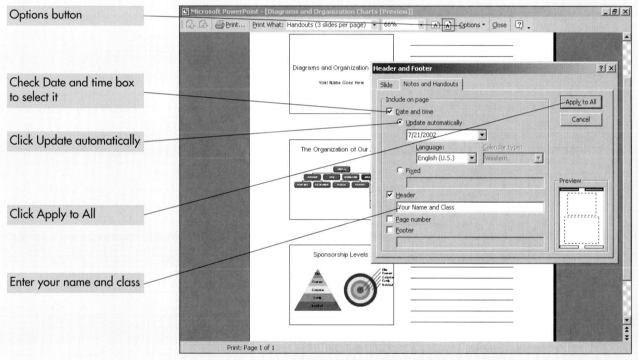

(g) Print the Audience Handouts (step 7)

FIGURE 3.5 *Hands-on Exercise 2 (continued)*

PRINT IN A VARIETY OF FORMATS

Use the flexibility inherent in the Print command to print a presentation in a variety of formats. Pull down the File menu, click the Print command to display the Print dialog box, and then select the desired output. Print handouts for your audience that contain the slide miniatures, or give your audience an outline containing the text of the entire presentation. Print the Notes Pages for yourself as a guide in preparing for the presentation. And finally, you can print the slides themselves, one per page, on overhead transparency masters as backup in case the computer is not available.

A *chart* (or graph) is a graphic representation of data. You can import an Excel chart into a PowerPoint presentation and/or you can create a chart from scratch. The latter is accomplished through **Microsoft Graph**, the default charting program for Microsoft Office that is installed automatically with PowerPoint. The program has many of the same capabilities as the charting component of Microsoft Excel.

All charts are based on numeric values called **data points** and descriptive entries called **category labels**. The data points are grouped into one or more **data series** that appear in rows or columns on the worksheet. This terminology is illustrated in Figure 3.6. The **datasheet** in Figure 3.6a contains 16 data points that are divided into four data series. The data represents revenue that has been raised through various funding sources in each of four quarters. Figure 3.6b displays the associated side-by-side column chart when the data series are plotted in rows. Figure 3.6c displays a comparable chart except that the data series are in columns.

Both charts plot a total of 16 data points (four revenue categories over four quarters), but they group the data differently. Figure 3.6b displays the data by quarter whereas Figure 3.6c displays the data by funding source. The choice between the two charts depends on your message and whether you want to emphasize revenue by quarter or by funding source. It sounds complicated, but it's not, and Microsoft Graph will create either chart for you according to your specifications.

- If you specify that the data series are in rows (Figure 3.6b), Microsoft Graph will
  - Use the first row in the datasheet for the category labels on the X axis.
  - Use the remaining rows for the four data series (each funding source represents a different series).
  - Use the first column for the legend text (the legend appears below the chart).
- If you specify that the data series are in columns (Figure 3.6c) the wizard will
  - Use the first column in the datasheet for the category labels on the X axis.
  - Use the remaining columns for the four data series (each quarter represents a different series).
  - Use the first row for the legend text (the legend appears below the chart).

Stacked Column Charts

Multiple data series are typically plotted as one of two chart types—**side-by-side column charts** or **stacked column charts**. Once again, the choice depends on the intended message. If, for example, you want to emphasize the individual revenue amounts in each quarter or revenue category, then the side-by-side columns in Figures 3.6b and 3.6c are more appropriate. If, on the other hand, you want to emphasize the total revenue for each quarter or category, the stacked columns in Figures 3.6d and 3.6e are preferable. The advantage of the stacked column is that the totals are clearly shown and can be easily compared. The disadvantage is that the segments within each column do not start at the same point, making it difficult to determine the actual sales for the individual categories.

Note, too, that the scale on the Y axis in the charts is different for charts with side-by-side columns versus charts with stacked columns. The side-by-side columns in Figure 3.6 show the revenue of each category or quarter, and so the Y axis goes only to $40,000. The stacked columns, however, reflect the total revenue in each quarter or category, and thus the scale goes to $90,000 or $120,000, respectively. Realize, too, that for a stacked column chart to make sense, its numbers must be additive; you shouldn't automatically convert a side-by-side column chart to its stacked column equivalent. It would not make sense, for example, to convert a column chart that plots unit sales and dollar sales side by side, to a stacked column chart that adds the two, because units and dollars represent different physical concepts, and do not make sense when added together.

Introduction to Charts - Datasheet

		A ⊞ 1st Qtr	B ⊞ 2nd Qtr	C ⊞ 3rd Qtr	D ⊞ 4th Qtr	E
1	Gift Shop	$9,000	$11,000	$13,000	$15,000	
2	Magazines	$8,000	$10,000	$13,000	$17,000	
3	Tours	$15,000	$24,000	$30,000	$39,000	
4	Seminars	$8,000	$10,000	$12,000	$14,000	
5						

(a) Datasheet

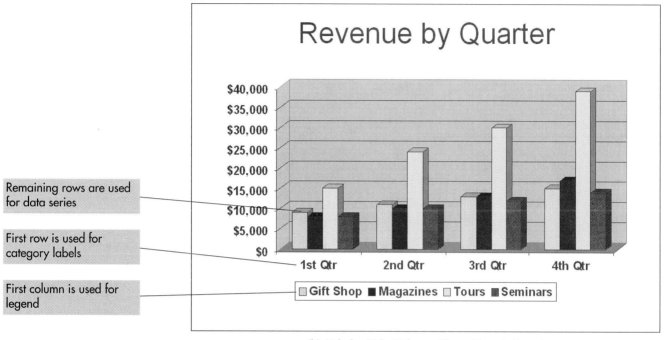

(b) Side-by-Side Column Chart (Data in Rows)

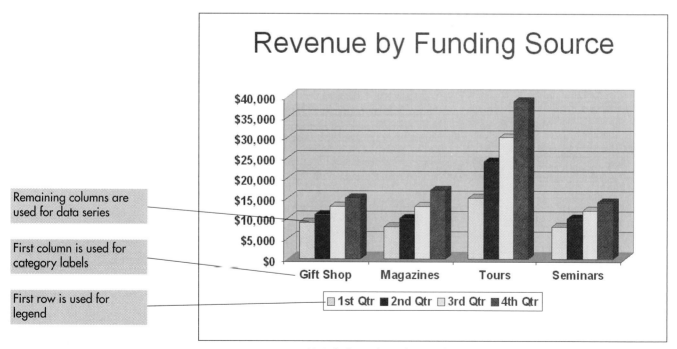

(c) Side-by-Side Column Chart (Data in Columns)

FIGURE 3.6 *Microsoft Graph*

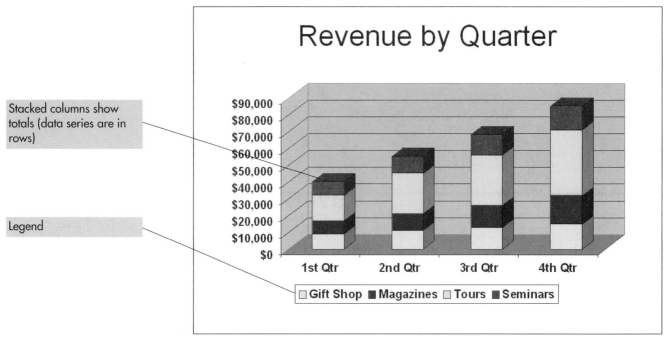

Stacked columns show totals (data series are in rows)

Legend

(d) Stacked Column Chart (Data in Rows)

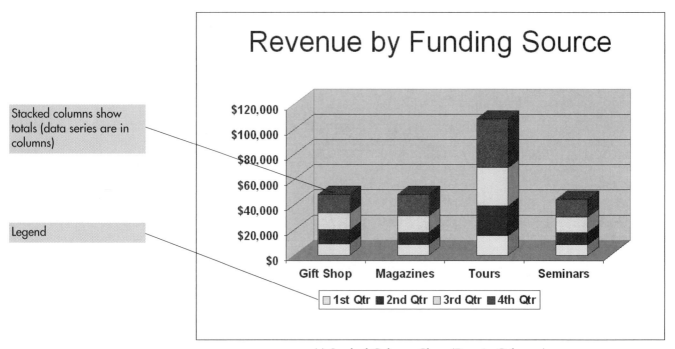

Stacked columns show totals (data series are in columns)

Legend

(e) Stacked Column Chart (Data in Columns)

FIGURE 3.6 *Microsoft Graph (continued)*

EMPHASIZE YOUR MESSAGE

A chart exists to deliver a message, and you want that message to be as clear as possible. One way to help put your point across is to choose a title that leads the audience. A neutral title such as *Revenue by Quarter* does nothing and requires the audience to reach its own conclusion. A better title might be *Our Revenues Are Growing,* which conveys an optimistic sense of a growing business.

MICROSOFT GRAPH

Objective   Use Microsoft Graph to insert a graph into a presentation; modify the graph to display the data in rows or columns; change the graph format and underlying data. Use Figure 3.7 as a guide in the exercise.

Step 1:   **Start Microsoft Graph**

➤ Start PowerPoint. Click the **New button** on the Standard toolbar to begin a new presentation. Enter the title **Introduction to Charts** and your name on the title slide. Save the presentation as **Introduction to Charts** in the **Exploring PowerPoint folder**.

➤ Click the **New Slide button** to insert a new slide. If necessary, click the **down arrow** at the top of the task pane and select **Slide Layout**. Scroll in the task pane until you can select (click) the **Title and Chart layout** as shown in Figure 3.7a. Close the task pane.

➤ Double click the icon to **add chart** to start Microsoft Graph.

New button

New Slide button

Double click to add chart

Double click Title and Chart layout

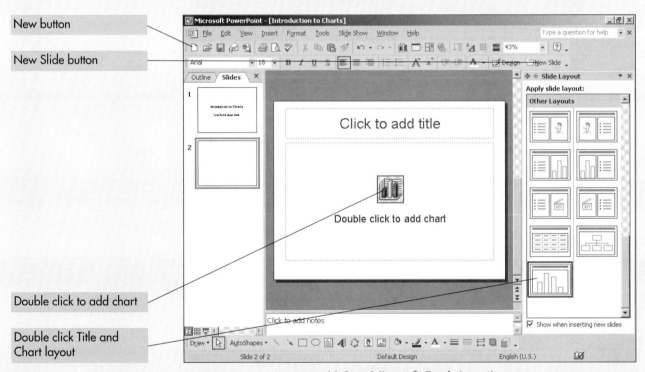

(a) Start Microsoft Graph (step 1)

FIGURE 3.7 *Hands-on Exercise 3*

INSERTING A CHART

There are several different ways to insert a chart into a presentation. You can insert a new slide and choose one of several slide layouts that contain a placeholder for a chart. You can pull down the Insert menu and select the Chart command, or you can click the Insert Chart button on the Standard toolbar. You can also link or embed a chart from an Excel workbook.

Step 2: **The Default Chart**

➤ The default datasheet and chart should be displayed on your monitor. The menus and toolbar have changed to reflect the Microsoft Graph application.

➤ Click and drag the **title bar** to move the datasheet so that you can see more of the chart, as shown in Figure 3.7b. Click and drag the borders of the datasheet to enlarge (shrink) the datasheet as appropriate. Do not be concerned if the values in your datasheet are different from those in the figure.

➤ Click in the cell containing "East". Type **Gift Shop** and press **enter**. The legend changes to reflect the new entry. (We complete the data entry in the next step.)

➤ Click the **View Datasheet button** on the (Microsoft Graph) Standard toolbar to close the datasheet. Click the **View Datasheet button** a second time to open the datasheet.

➤ Click the **Legend button** on the Standard toolbar to suppress the legend on the graph. Click the **Legend button** a second time to display the legend.

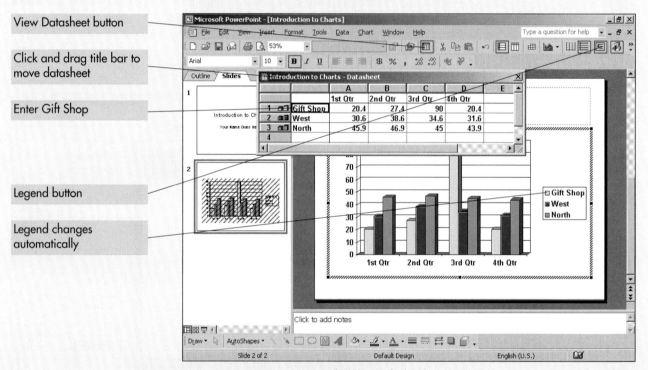

(b) The Default Chart (step 2)

FIGURE 3.7   *Hands-on Exercise 3*

IMPORT THE DATA

Microsoft Graph enables you to import data from Microsoft Excel and use that data as the basis for the chart. (You should know the name of the workbook, the appropriate worksheet in that workbook, and the cell range in that worksheet prior to importing the data.) Start Microsoft Graph, click in the upper left square (the area above row 1 and to the left of column A) to select the entire datasheet, then click the Import File button on the Microsoft Graph toolbar to display the Import File dialog box. Select the appropriate drive and folder containing the workbook you want to import, select the file, specify the worksheet and associated range, then click OK. (See practice exercise 6 at the end of the chapter.)

Step 3:   **Change the Data**

> Close the left pane and give yourself more room in which to work. (You can reopen the left pane at any time by clicking the **Normal View button** above the status bar.) Double click on the graph.
> Click in cell **A1**, the cell containing the gift shop data for the first quarter. Type **9000** and press the **Tab** or **right arrow key** to move to cell B1. The chart changes automatically to reflect the new data.
> Complete the data for the first data series (**Gift Shop**). Enter data for the next two series, (**Magazines** and **Tours**) as shown in Figure 3.7c. Enter data for the fourth series (**Seminars**) to complete the datasheet.
> Click and drag to select all of the numeric data as shown in Figure 3.7c. Click the **Currency Style button** to display a dollar sign next to each value, then click the **Decrease Decimal button** twice to eliminate the cents. Adjust the column width as necessary.
> Check that all of the values in your datasheet match those in the Figure 3.7c. Close the datasheet. Save the presentation.

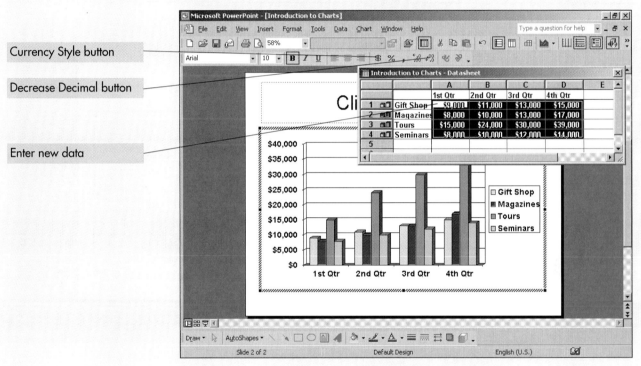

(c) Change the Data (step 3)

FIGURE 3.7   *Hands-on Exercise 3 (continued)*

REMOVING (HIDING) A DATA SERIES

Open the datasheet, click the row number or column header of the data series you want to delete, and press the Del key. The series disappears from both the datasheet and the associated chart. Alternatively, you can leave the data series in the datasheet, but can exclude (hide) it from the chart. Click the row number or column header to select the data series, pull down the Data menu, and select the Exclude Row/Column command. To restore the data series in the graph, select the series, pull down the Data menu, and select the Include Row/Column command.

Step 4:   **Change the Orientation and Chart Type**

➤ Click the **By Column button** on the Standard toolbar to change the data series from rows to columns as shown in Figure 3.7d. The X axis changes to display the funding sources. The legend indicates the quarter.

➤ Click the **By Row button** on the Standard toolbar to change the data series back to rows. Click the **By Column button** a second time to match the orientation in Figure 3.7d.

➤ Pull down the **Chart menu** and click **Chart Type** to display the associated dialog box. Click the **Standard Types tab**, click **Column**, then select **Stacked column with a 3-D visual effect**.

➤ Check the box to preserve the **Default formatting**. Click **OK** to accept the settings and close the dialog box.

➤ The chart changes to a stacked column chart, which more clearly shows the total revenue from each funding source.

➤ Save the presentation.

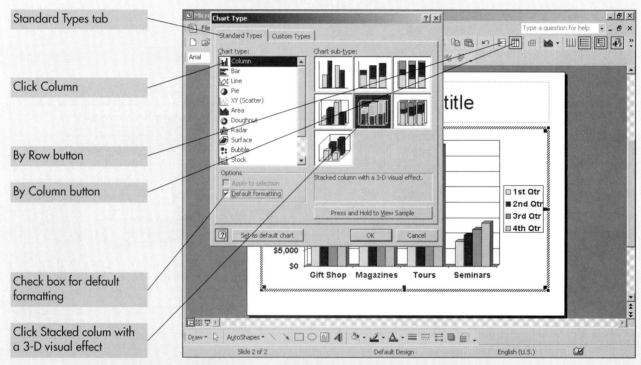

Standard Types tab

Click Column

By Row button

By Column button

Check box for default formatting

Click Stacked colum with a 3-D visual effect

(d) Change the Orientation and Chart Type (step 4)

FIGURE 3.7   *Hands-on Exercise 3 (continued)*

TO CLICK OR DOUBLE CLICK

Once created, a chart becomes an object in a presentation that retains its connection to Microsoft Graph for easy editing. Click any object on the slide other than the chart to deselect the chart. Now click the chart once to select the chart and display the conventional sizing handles to move or size the chart just as you would any Windows object. Double click the chart (it will be surrounded with a hashed border) to restart Microsoft Graph in order to edit the chart.

Step 5:   **Complete the Chart**

➤ The chart should still be selected. Pull down the **Chart menu**, click the **Chart Options command** to display the associated dialog box, then click the **Legend tab**.
➤ Click the option to display the legend on the **Bottom**, then click **OK**.
➤ **Right click** the top section on any stacked column to display a context-sensitive menu and click the command to **Format Data Series** to display the associated dialog box.
➤ Click the **Patterns tab**, click **Red**, then click **OK** to change the color of this data series (the amounts for the fourth quarter) to **red**. Change the color of the next data series (the 3rd quarter) to **yellow**.
➤ Click outside the hashed area, then click in the title placeholder to enter the title of the slide, **Revenue by Funding Source**, as shown in Figure 3.7e.
➤ Save the presentation.

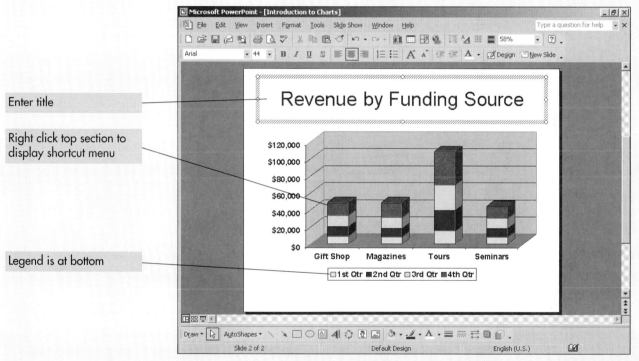

(e) Complete the Chart (step 5)

FIGURE 3.7   *Hands-on Exercise 3 (continued)*

SET A TIME LIMIT

Microsoft Graph gives you (almost too much) control over the appearance of a chart. Save the presentation before you begin, then use the Format Data Series command to change the color, shape, pattern and/or add labels to columns within a chart. Use the Undo command if the results are different from what you expected. (If the Undo command is inoperative, you can always use the Chart Options command to return to the default formatting.) It is fun to experiment, but set a time limit and stick to it! Remember, too, that the type of chart is more important than the formatting.

Step 6: **Copy the Chart**

➤ Click the **Normal button** to restore the left pane in Figure 3.7f. Click (select) the slide containing the chart. Click the **Copy button** (or press **Ctrl+C**) to copy the slide to the clipboard.

➤ Click the **Paste button** (or press **Ctrl+V**) to complete the copy operation. The presentation should contain two identical charts. We will now modify the copied chart by changing its orientation.

➤ Select (click) the third slide if necessary. Double click the chart to start Microsoft Graph, then click the **By Row button** to display the data series by rows. The name of each quarter appears on the X axis, and the funding sources appear in the legend as shown in Figure 3.7f.

➤ Click outside the chart area, then click in the placeholder for the title. Change the title to **Our Revenues Are Growing**.

➤ Print the completed presentation for your instructor (print the slides as handouts, with three slides per page).

➤ Save the presentation. Exit PowerPoint if you do not want to continue with the next exercise at this time.

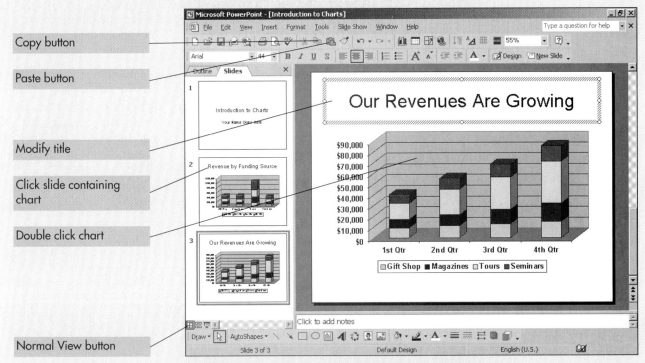

Copy button

Paste button

Modify title

Click slide containing chart

Double click chart

Normal View button

(f) Copy the Chart (step 6)

FIGURE 3.7 *Hands-on Exercise 3 (continued)*

DON'T FORGET HELP

Microsoft Graph includes its own Help system, which functions identically to the Help system in any other application. Pull down the Help menu and search on any topic for which you want additional information. Remember, too, that you can print the contents of a help screen by pulling down the File menu and selecting the Print Topic command.

Custom animation determines when and how objects appear on a slide, what they do after they appear on the screen, and how the objects are to exit. It's difficult to describe animation on a static page, but we do our best in Figure 3.8. The sequence begins in Figure 3.8a with the appearance of the title and giraffe, who walks across the screen in Figure 3.8b, after which the author's name appears on the slide. The giraffe makes his exit in Figure 3.8c, and the author's name increases in size.

The animation is accomplished through the effects specified in the task pane of Figure 3.8d. The icons are color coded—green, red, and yellow to indicate an **entrance effect**, an **exit effect**, and an **emphasis effect**, respectively. The custom animation for the title is selected. The effect is "fly in," which starts on a mouse click. The object enters from the top at medium speed. Look closely and you will see a Mouse icon next to the selected animation within the task pane. Look further and you see a Clock icon next to all subsequent animations to indicate that the animations take place automatically one after another. The **advanced timeline** shows the sequence and duration of each effect.

(a) Giraffe Entering

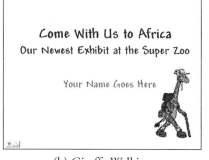

(b) Giraffe Walking

(c) Ending Slide

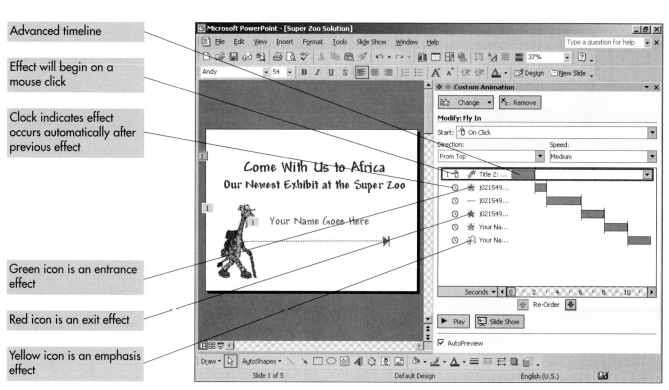

(d) Custom Animation Task Pane

FIGURE 3.8 *Custom Animation (Title Slide)*

Figure 3.9 displays an animation series in conjunction with a chart. The various categories (the stacked columns) appear sequentially upon a series of mouse clicks, after which the title increases in size. Figure 3.9a shows the slide with just the title, Figure 3.9b shows the slide after two columns have appeared, and Figure 3.9c shows the completed slide, with an enlarged title. The corresponding animation task pane is shown in Figure 3.9d.

The Mouse icons within the task pane indicate that the entrance of each column (category) takes place in conjunction with a mouse click. (The Clock icon next to the title object, however, indicates that this effect follows automatically after the previous effect. Note, too, that the entire chart is animated with a single command, in which you specify that the chart animation is to take place by category, rather than as a single object.

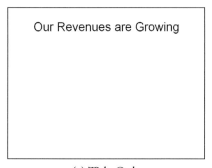

(a) Title Only

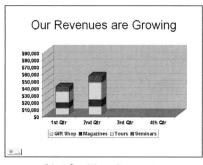

(b) After Two Categories

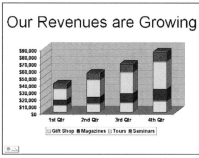

(c) Ending Slide

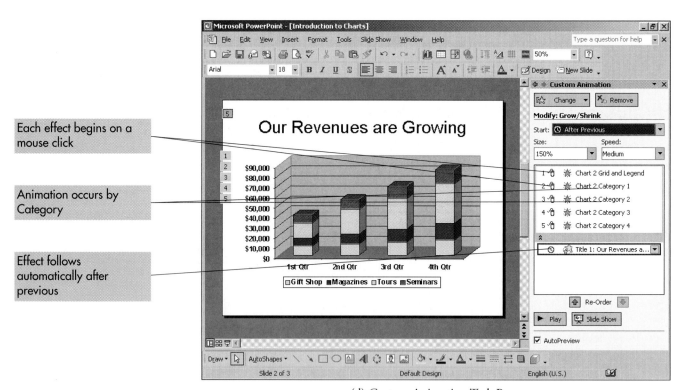

(d) Custom Animation Task Pane

FIGURE 3.9 *Custom Animation (The Chart)*

CUSTOM ANIMATION

Objective   Add custom animation to individual objects on a slide; use custom animation to animate an organization chart and a graphical chart.

Step 1:   **Insert a Slide**

➤ Start PowerPoint. Open the **Super Zoo presentation** in the **Exploring PowerPoint folder**. Add your name to the title slide.

➤ Pull down the **Insert menu**, click the **Slides from Files command** to display the Slide Finder dialog box in Figure 3.10a.

➤ Click the **Browse button** and open the **Diagrams and Organization Charts presentation** from the first hands-on exercise. Select the **organization chart**, then click the **Insert button** to insert this slide into the presentation.

➤ Click the **Browse button** a second time, but this time select the **Introduction to Charts presentation** from the second exercise. Insert the chart that plots **revenue by quarter** (the second chart). Close the Slide Finder dialog box.

➤ Save the presentation as **Super Zoo Solution** in the **Exploring PowerPoint folder**.

Browse button

Select Diagrams and Organization Charts presentations

Click Slide 2

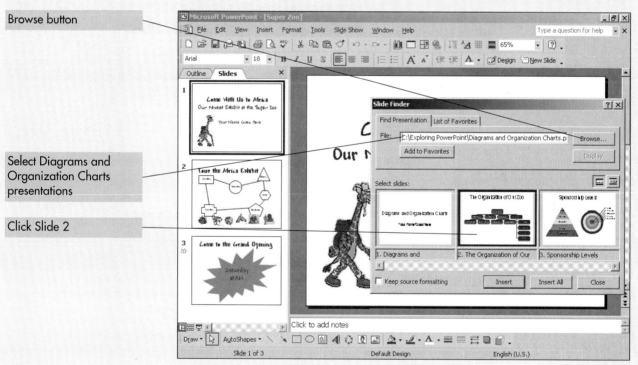

(a) Insert a Slide (step 1)

FIGURE 3.10   *Hands-on Exercise 4*

CREATE A NEW FOLDER

Pull down the File menu, click the Open or Save As command as appropriate, then click the Create New Folder button to display the New Folder dialog box. Enter the name of the new folder, then click OK. Use the Look In box to change to the new folder the next time you open a document.

Step 2:   **Animate the Title Slide**

➤ The font for the slide titles of the newly inserted slides does not match the font on the title slide. Use the **Format Painter** to copy the font (**Andy, 54-point, blue**) from the title slide to the inserted slides.

➤ Select the title slide. Pull down the **Slide Show menu** and click the **Custom Animation command** to open the task pane as shown in Figure 3.10b.

➤ Click anywhere in the title to select the title. Click the **Add Effect button** in the task pane, click **Entrance**, and click the **Fly In** effect. The title flies in from the bottom of the slide (the default position).

➤ Modify the parameters for the Fly In effect by clicking the **down arrows** in the appropriate list boxes. Set the direction to **From Top** and the speed to **Medium**. Click the **Play button** to see how these parameters modify the animation.

➤ Select the **giraffe**. Click the **Add Effect button**, choose the **Dissolve In** entrance effect, change the start to **After Previous**, and set the speed to **Fast**. A second effect appears in the task pane.

➤ Save the presentation.

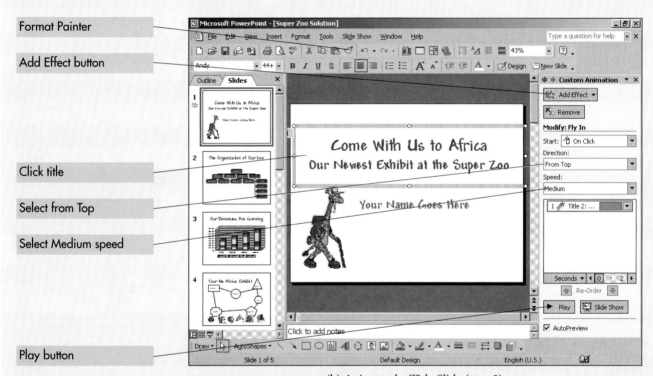

Format Painter

Add Effect button

Click title

Select from Top

Select Medium speed

Play button

(b) Animate the Title Slide (step 2)

FIGURE 3.10   *Hands-on Exercise 4 (continued)*

YOU'RE THE DIRECTOR

No one ever said that animating a presentation was quick or easy. It takes time, more time than you might expect initially, as each slide has to be choreographed in detail. Think of yourself as the director who must tell the actors (the objects on a slide) when to come on stage and how to make their entrance. Try to think of the overall performance, and then develop one object at a time. Save the presentation continually as you add new effects. Click the Undo command anytime the result is not what you intended it to be.

Step 3   **Complete the Animation**

➤ Close the left pane to give yourself more room in which to work as shown in Figure 3.10c. Add the animation effects in the order below. Set each effect to start **After Previous effect**:
  • A **motion path to the right** for the giraffe at **slow speed**. (You will have to increase the length of the motion path by dragging the red arrow to the right.)
  • The giraffe should **dissolve out** (exit effect) at a **medium speed**.
  • Your name should dissolve in at **medium speed**.
  • Your name should **grow 150 percent** (emphasis effect) at **medium speed**.
➤ Click the **down arrow** on the last effect in the task pane. Set the option to show the **Advanced timeline**, then click the **left arrow** below the timeline so that you see the entire sequence. (Increase the width of the task pane to see the timeline more clearly.)
➤ Select the first effect, then click the **Play button** to view the animation for the entire slide. (You can modify any existing effect by selecting the effect in the task pane, and clicking the **Change button**.)
➤ Save the presentation.

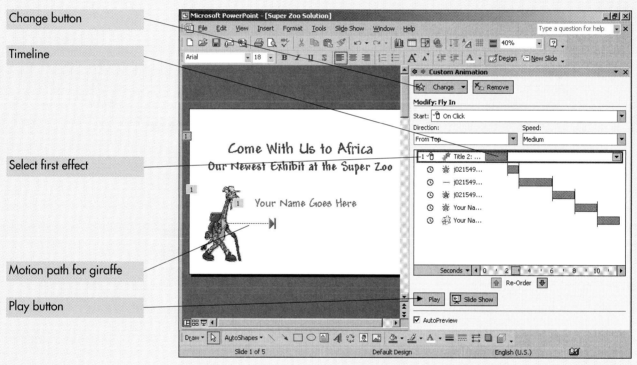

(c) Complete the Animation (step 3)

FIGURE 3.10   *Hands-on Exercise 4 (continued)*

THE CUSTOM ANIMATION TASK PANE

The icon next to each effect in the custom animation task pane indicates when the effect is to appear within the animation sequence. A Mouse icon indicates that the effect begins with a mouse click, whereas the Clock icon shows that the effect will appear automatically after the previous effect. The absence of an icon means that the effect will start simultaneously with the previous effect. Note, too, that the various effects are color coded, where green, red, and yellow, denote an entrance, exit, and emphasis effect, respectively.

Step 4: **Animate the Organization Chart**

➤ Press the **PgDn key** to move to the second slide (the slide with the organization chart). Click the **Text Box tool** on the Drawing toolbar, then click and drag to create a text box at the bottom of the slide.

➤ Enter the text of the box "**And Our Newest Exhibit . . .** " as shown in Figure 3.10d. Change the font to match the font on the title of the slide, albeit in a smaller point size.

➤ Open the Custom Animation task pane. Select the text box, and then add the **Fade entrance effect**, at **Medium speed**, to begin **After Previous effect**. Now click anywhere in the organization chart to make it the active object, and add the **Fade entrance effect**.

➤ Click the **down arrow** next to the Organization Chart animation in the task pane. Click **Effect Options** to display the Fade dialog box as shown in Figure 3.10d, then click the **Diagram Animation tab**. Click the **down arrow** in the Group diagram list box, select **Each branch, shape by shape**, and click **OK**.

➤ The Organization Chart animation should be selected. Change the start of the animation to **After Previous**. Click the **Play button** to see the animation thus far.

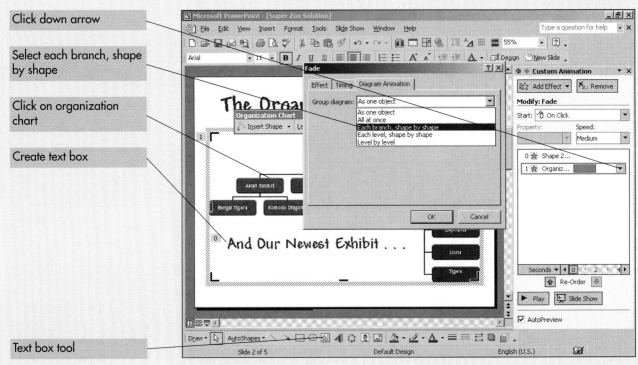

(d) Animate the Organization Chart (step 4)

FIGURE 3.10 *Hands-on Exercise 4 (continued)*

ANIMATING DIAGRAMS

Each shape in an organization chart requires its own animation effect if the shapes are to appear individually. You do not, however, have to apply the effects individually. Select the entire chart and apply an entrance effect, then go to the animation task pane, click the arrow on effect, click the Effect Options command, click the Diagram Animation tab, and choose the type of animation. You can animate each branch shape by shape or each level shape by shape.

Step 5: **Change the Animation Sequence**

➤ We will change the animation sequence, so that the text announcing the new exhibit appears prior to the entrance of the associated branch in the organization chart.

➤ Click the **double arrow (chevron)** in the animation pane. The single effect for the chart expands to display the animation of the individual boxes as shown in Figure 3.10e.

➤ Select the animation effect for **Shape 29** (the number on your text box may be different from ours).

➤ Click the **Reorder down arrow** repeatedly until this effect is immediately above the **African Exhibit**. Click the **Play button** to test the presentation.

➤ The blocks in the organization chart should come in sequentially (top to bottom, one branch at a time), until you see the box for **Koala Bears**.

➤ You should then see the text for the newest exhibit, after which you will see the branch for the **African exhibit**.

➤ Save the presentation.

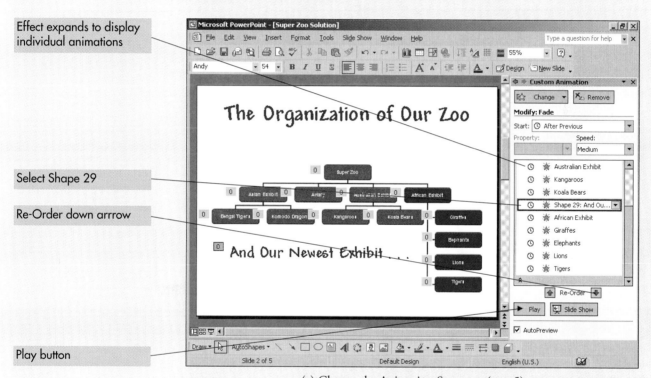

(e) Change the Animation Sequence (step 5)

FIGURE 3.10 *Hands-on Exercise 4 (continued)*

DELETE THE EFFECT NOT THE OBJECT

Click any object on a slide to select the object and display the associated sizing handles. This action also selects the associated animation effect (if any) in the custom animation task pane by surrounding the descriptive text with a rectangle. Be careful, however, about pressing the Del key; pressing the Del key when the object is selected deletes both the object and the animation affect. To delete the animation, but retain the object, click off (deselect) the object, click (select) the animation effect, then press the Del key. Use the Undo command if you make a mistake and try again.

Step 6:   **Animate the Chart**

➤ Press the **PgDn key** to move to the slide containing the chart. Select the chart.
➤ Click the **Add Effect button** in the task pane and choose the **Fade entrance effect** at **Medium speed**.
➤ Click the **down arrow** next to the chart animation in the task pane, click **Effect Options** to display the Fade dialog box, and click the **Chart Animation tab**. Click the **down arrow** in the Group chart list box and select **By Category**.
➤ Clear the box to **animate the grid and legend**. Click **OK**. You should see the columns appear one at a time as the effect is previewed automatically. Click the **chevron** in the animation task pane to see the individual animations.
➤ Select the title of the slide. Click the **Add effect button**, select **Emphasis**, and then choose the **Grow/Shrink effect** as shown in Figure 3.10f. The default setting is to increase the font size 150%.
➤ Save the presentation.

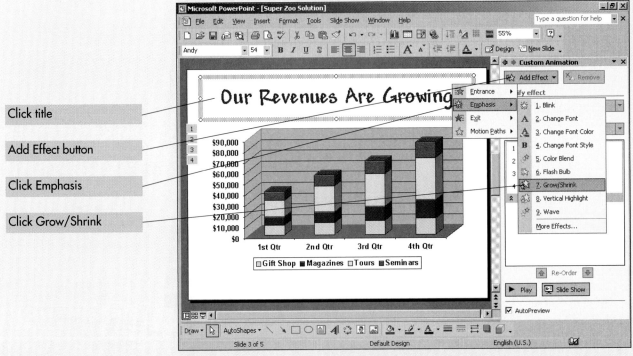

(f) Animate the Chart (step 6)

FIGURE 3.10   *Hands-on Exercise 4 (continued)*

CATEGORY VERSUS SERIES

Choose the effect that will best convey your intended message. Animating by category displays the stacked columns one column at a time, focusing on the difference between columns. Animating by series displays one element at a time from every column, emphasizing the growth of each column. Note, too, that the ability to animate a chart by its components exists only for charts created by Microsoft Graph; you cannot animate a chart that was imported from Microsoft Excel.

Step 7: **Animate Multiple Objects**

➤ Press the **PgDn key** to move to the next slide. Press and hold the **Shift** (or **Ctrl**) **key** as you click the multiple clip art images that are on the slide.

➤ Click the **Add Effect button**, click **Entrance**, then click **Random Effects** to apply a different effect to each of the selected objects. The effects have been created, but you still have to set the timing.

➤ The first effect is set to begin on a mouse click. Press and hold the **Ctrl key** as you select every effect but the first. Click the **down arrow** next to the Start list box in the animation task pane. Choose **After Previous** as shown in Figure 3.10g.

➤ Click and drag each animal to its appropriate place on the slide. Click the **Play button** to test the animation. Save the presentation.

➤ Click the **Slide Show button**, then click the mouse to begin the animation. Note the movement within the elephant and lion after these (animated GIF) objects appear on the screen. Press **Esc** to cancel the show and continue working.

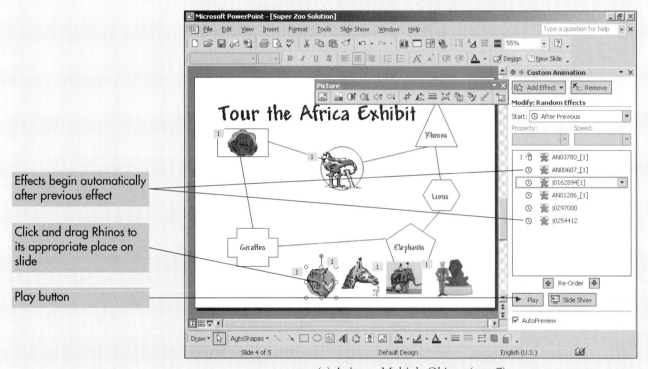

Effects begin automatically after previous effect

Click and drag Rhinos to its appropriate place on slide

Play button

(g) Animate Multiple Objects (step 7)

FIGURE 3.10   *Hands-on Exercise 4 (continued)*

USE ANIMATED GIFS

An animated GIF file, as its name implies, adds motion to the associated clip art. Click the Insert Clip Art button on the Drawing toolbar to open the task pane. Click the down arrow in the Results Should be list box, then clear the check boxes next to all four major categories: clip art, photographs, movies, and sound. Look at the list of movie file types and check the box for an animated GIF file. Click in the Search text box, type "animal", then click the Search button to look for animated GIF files related to animals. Remember to reset the search criteria (i.e., check the high-level box for all media types) the next time you insert clip art.

Step 8: **Create the Explosion**

➤ Press the **PgDn key** to move to the last slide. Click in the left pane, click the down arrow in the **Zoom box**, and change the magnification to **37%**. You may be surprised to see that there is an AutoShape above the actual slide as shown in Figure 3.10h.

➤ The animation effects for this object have been set. The object will zoom in from the screen center, at a very fast speed, to the sound of an explosion, automatically after the previous effect.

➤ Select the **AutoShape**, click the **Copy button**, then click the **Paste button** to duplicate the shape. The animation effects are copied with the object.

➤ Click and drag the copied shape away from the original, then click and drag a sizing handle to change its size. Click the **Fill button** on the Drawing toolbar to change its color. Repeat this process to create 10 to 20 similar AutoShapes around the slide.

➤ Click the **Play button** to see the completed animation. Experiment with a different sound and/or a different timing for some of the shapes.

➤ Save the presentation.

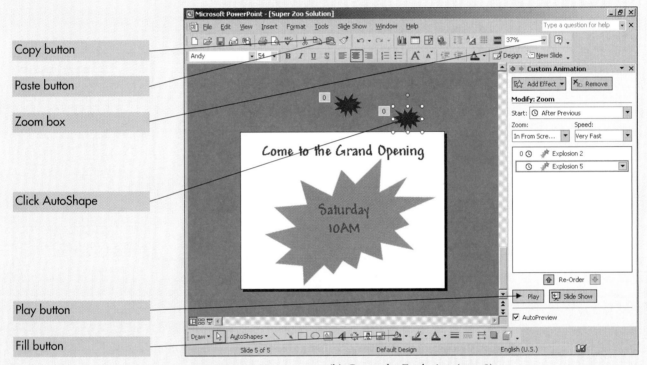

(h) Create the Explosion (step 8)

FIGURE 3.10 *Hands-on Exercise 4 (continued)*

COPY EFFICIENTLY

You start with one object and need a total of 15. You can copy and paste the individual object multiple times, or you can duplicate groups of objects. Copy the first object, then press and hold the Ctrl key to select both objects. Press Ctrl+C to copy, then Ctrl+V to paste. You now have four objects. Click and drag the copied objects to position them on the screen (you may want to select the objects individually). Now select and copy all four objects to get eight, then copy the eight and so on.

Step 9: **Show Time**

> Close the animation task pane. Change to the **Slide Sorter view**, where you should see five slides in the completed presentation. (The AutoShapes in the ending slide do not appear in this view, because they are off the slide.)

> Select the first slide, and click the **Slide Show button**. The screen is blank.

- Click the mouse, the title appears, the giraffe walks across the screen in Figure 3.10i, and then your name appears.
- Click the mouse to move to the next slide and see the animation for the organization chart. Click the mouse to move to the next slide.
- You should see an empty chart because we opted not to animate the grid or legend. Click the mouse repeatedly to display the stacked columns for each series, then click the mouse a final time to enlarge the title. Click the mouse to move to the next slide.
- Click the mouse to display the animals as you tour the **Africa exhibit**. Click the mouse when you are ready to move to the last slide.
- The fireworks begin immediately. Press **Esc** when the presentation ends.

> Exit PowerPoint. Congratulations on a job well done.

The giraffe walks across the screen

(i) Show Time (step 9)

FIGURE 3.10 *Hands-on Exercise 4 (continued)*

THE MEETING MINDER

Use the Meeting Minder to keep track of issues that arise during a presentation in order to create a "To Do" list for future sessions. Right click any slide during the presentation, click the Meeting Minder command to display the associated dialog box, then click the Action Items tab. Enter the appropriate information, then click the Add button. Continue with the presentation, which now contains an ending slide, "Action Items", that displays the information you entered through the Meeting Minder.

A photo album imports multiple photographs into a presentation, without having to format each picture individually. The photos may be taken from a hard disk, a scanner, or a digital camera. Photographs may also be inserted individually into a presentation and subsequently cropped if necessary. (The Photo Album command disables cropping.)

The Joint Photographic Experts Group (JPG, pronounced "jpeg") format is the most common file type for photographs. The Graphics Interchange Format (GIF, pronounced "jif") is used for clip art and similar images.

The Diagram Gallery provides six figure types to describe different types of relationships within an organization. The diagrams include an organization chart (hierarchical relationships), a cycle diagram (continuous cycle), a radial diagram (elements around a core), a pyramid diagram (foundation relationships), a target diagram (steps toward a goal), and a Venn diagram (overlap between elements).

All diagrams are developed within the drawing canvas (an area enclosed within hashed lines) that appears automatically as you create a diagram. Additional (e.g., subordinate) shapes can be inserted, and/or existing shapes can be deleted. The appearance of the diagram as a whole can be changed through the AutoFormat command, and/or individual shapes can be formatted independently.

A chart (or graph) is a graphic representation of data that is based on numeric values called data points and descriptive entries called category labels. The data points are grouped into one or more data series that appear in rows or columns of a spreadsheet. Multiple data series are typically plotted as one of two chart types—side-by-side column charts or stacked column charts. The choice between plotting data in rows or columns, as well as the decision on the type of chart, depends on the intended message. An Excel chart can be imported into a PowerPoint presentation, and/or it can be created within the presentation. The latter is accomplished through Microsoft Graph, the default charting program for Microsoft Office that is installed automatically with PowerPoint.

Custom animation determines when and how objects appear on a slide, what they do after they appear on the screen, and how the objects are to exit. The animation is accomplished in the custom animation task pane. The icons in the task pane are color coded—green, red, and yellow to indicate an entrance effect, an exit effect, and an emphasis effect, respectively. The advanced timeline shows the sequence and duration of each effect. Custom animation may be applied to charts and/or organization charts to display the series, branches, or levels, individually, as opposed to displaying the entire object at one time.

KEY TERMS

Advanced timeline (p. 153)
Animation (p. 124)
AutoFormat tool (p. 135)
Category labels (p. 144)
Chart (p. 144)
Crop tool (p. 122)
Custom animation (p. 124)
Cycle diagram (p. 135)
Data points (p. 144)
Data series (p. 144)
Datasheet (p. 144)
Diagram Gallery (p. 135)

Drawing canvas (p. 135)
Emphasis effect (p. 153)
Entrance effect (p. 153)
Exit effect (p. 153)
Format Background command
   (p. 122)
Format WordArt command (p. 122)
GIF format (p. 122)
JPEG format (p. 122)
Microsoft Graph (p. 144)
My Pictures Folder (p. 122)

Organization Chart (p. 135)
Photo album (p. 122)
Picture toolbar (p. 122)
Pyramid diagram (p. 135)
Radial diagram (p. 135)
Side-by-side column charts (p. 144)
Stacked column charts (p. 144)
Target diagram (p. 135)
Transition (p. 124)
Venn diagram (p. 135)

1. Which diagram type is recommended to show hierarchical relationships?
   (a) Organization chart
   (b) Pyramid diagram
   (c) Venn diagram
   (d) Radial diagram

2. You have created an organization chart with two levels. The president is at the top and there are three vice presidents. How do you add a fourth vice president?
   (a) Click in the President box and add an assistant
   (b) Click in the rightmost vice president's box and add a coworker
   (c) Both (a) and (b)
   (d) Neither (a) nor (b)

3. Which of the following best describes the formatting options for a diagram?
   (a) The entire diagram can be formatted as a single object using AutoFormat
   (b) Individual shapes can be selected and formatted independently
   (c) Both (a) and (b)
   (d) Neither (a) nor (b)

4. Which of the following *cannot* be accomplished using the Change to button on the Diagram toolbar?
   (a) Change an organization chart to a cycle diagram
   (b) Change a cycle diagram to a radial diagram
   (c) Change a radial diagram to a pyramid diagram
   (d) Change a pyramid diagram to a Venn diagram

5. Which of the following is true regarding custom animation?
   (a) An object may have an entrance effect but not an exit effect
   (b) An object may have an exit effect but not an entrance effect
   (c) An object may have both an entrance effect and an exit effect
   (d) An object may have neither an entrance effect nor an exit effect

6. Which of the following best describes the colors associated with custom animation effects?
   (a) Red, green, and yellow for entrance, exit, and emphasis, respectively
   (b) Red, yellow, and green for entrance, exit, and emphasis, respectively
   (c) Green, red, and yellow for entrance, exit, and emphasis, respectively
   (d) Green, yellow, and red for entrance, exit, and emphasis, respectively

7. Which of the following parameters is *not* specified in conjunction with the "Fly in" entrance effect?
   (a) The direction (e.g., top or bottom)
   (b) The speed (e.g., fast or slow)
   (c) The starting point (e.g., on a mouse click or after the previous animation)
   (d) The exit path

8. Which of the following animations is available for an organization chart?
   (a) A branch at a time and shape by shape within the branch
   (b) A level at a time and shape by shape within the level
   (c) As a single object (the entire chart comes in at once)
   (d) All of the above

9. What happens if you click the View Datasheet button on the Microsoft Graph toolbar twice in a row?
   (a) The datasheet is closed (hidden)
   (b) The datasheet is opened (displayed)
   (c) The datasheet is in the same status as it was before it was clicked
   (d) Impossible to determine

10. Which of the following is true of data series that are plotted in rows?
    (a) The first row in the datasheet contains the category names for the X axis
    (b) The first column in the datasheet contains the legend
    (c) Both (a) and (b)
    (d) Neither (a) nor (b)

11. Which of the following is true of data series that are plotted in columns?
    (a) The first column in the datasheet contains the category names for the X axis
    (b) The first row in the datasheet contains the legend
    (c) Both (a) and (b)
    (d) Neither (a) nor (b)

12. How do you create a new slide containing a chart?
    (a) Add a blank slide, pull down the Insert menu, and click the Chart command
    (b) Add a blank slide, then click the Insert Chart button on the Standard toolbar
    (c) Add a blank slide, select a slide layout that contains a chart, then double click the placeholder for the chart in the Slide view
    (d) All of the above

13. Which effect will display the columns in a stacked column chart one at a time?
    (a) Animation by series
    (b) Animation by category
    (c) Animation by elements in a series
    (d) Animation by elements in a category

14. Custom Animation enables you to:
    (a) Specify a different animation effect for each object on a slide
    (b) Change the order in which the objects appear on a slide
    (c) Both (a) and (b)
    (d) Neither (a) nor (b)

15. You are working on an organization chart. The hashed border surrounds the drawing canvas, but none of the objects in the chart is selected. What happens if you press the Del key?
    (a) The entire organization chart is deleted
    (b) The slide itself is deleted
    (c) The last box selected is deleted
    (d) Nothing, since no objects are selected within the drawing area

16. Which of the following *cannot* be accomplished directly by using the Format Photo Album command?
    (a) Changing the number of photographs on a slide
    (b) Changing the shape of the photographs
    (c) Inserting captions below the photographs
    (d) Adding custom animation to the individual photos

ANSWERS

1. a	**5.** c	**9.** c	**13.** b
2. b	**6.** c	**10.** c	**14.** c
3. c	**7.** d	**11.** c	**15.** a
4. a	**8.** d	**12.** d	**16.** d

1. Animation 101: You will find a partially completed version of the presentation in Figure 3.11 in the file *Chapter 3 Practice 1* in the Exploring PowerPoint folder. Open the presentation and add the indicated animation effects on each slide. Be sure to include a sound effect where indicated. Use any trigger that you deem appropriate; i.e., you can specify that the effect begins on a mouse click or after the previous effect as you see fit.

   a. Add your name on the title slide. The slide title should fly in from the top to the accompaniment of a drum roll.

   b. Slide two illustrates different entrance effects, each of which is denoted by a green icon in the custom animation task pane. Add sound where indicated, such as the whoosh for the last bullet.

   c. Slide three shows different ways to add emphasis to text. Note the specification of a typewriter sound for the last effect, which displays the letters one at a time

   d. Slide four contains various effects for emphasis. Once again, you have a sound effect, this time a gentle breeze.

   e. Slide five illustrates how to create motion paths.

   f. Slide six contains exit strategies.

   g. Save the completed presentation. Print the title slide as a full slide to use as a cover sheet for the assignment. Print the audience handouts of the revised presentation (six slides in all) for your instructor.

   h. View the completed presentation. Do you have a better appreciation for custom animation? Summarize your thoughts in a brief note to your instructor. Be sure to mention the different colors that are associated with entrance and exit effects. Describe the timeline and the associated icons that show when an object appears.

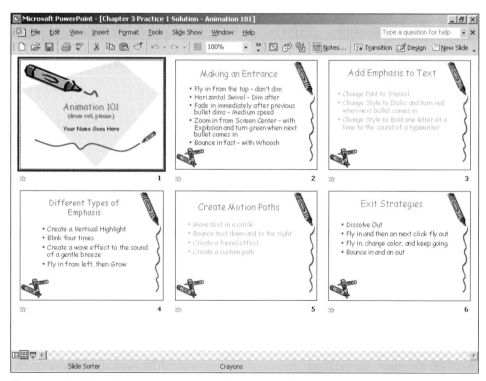

FIGURE 3.11   *Animation 101 (Exercise 1)*

BUILDS ON

HANDS-ON
EXERCISE 4
PAGES 155–163

2. Adding a Timeline: Create a new slide containing the timeline in Figure 3.12 for the existing Super Zoo presentation from the third hands-on exercise. You do not have to duplicate our slide exactly, but you are required to include the equivalent functionality.

   a. Open the Super Zoo presentation from the last hands-on exercise. Insert a new (title only) slide as the fourth slide in the presentation (i.e., insert the new slide after the stacked column chart). Add the title of the slide as shown in the figure.

   b. Click the Insert Table tool on the Standard toolbar to create a 2 x 12 (2 rows and 12 columns) table as shown in Figure 3.12. Click and drag the line separating the two rows in the table so that the top row is much narrower than the bottom. Click in the second row, then press enter two or three times to increase row size.

   c. Enter the months of the year in the top row. Format the text for January, as you see fit, then use the Format Painter to copy the formatting to the remaining months.

   d. Click the AutoShapes tool on the Drawing toolbar, choose Block Arrows, and create the first arrow. Right click the arrow and click the command to add text, then enter the appropriate text as shown in the figure.

   e. Copy this arrow (or create additional arrows) so that you have four milestones on the slide. Edit the text in each arrow as necessary. Use the same formatting for all four arrows.

   f. Insert an appropriate clip art image under each arrow.

   g. Animate the completed slide so that the individual milestones appear on successive mouse clicks. Use any effects that you deem appropriate.

   h. Print the title slide as a full slide to use as a cover sheet for the assignment. Print the audience handouts of the revised presentation (six slides in all) for your instructor.

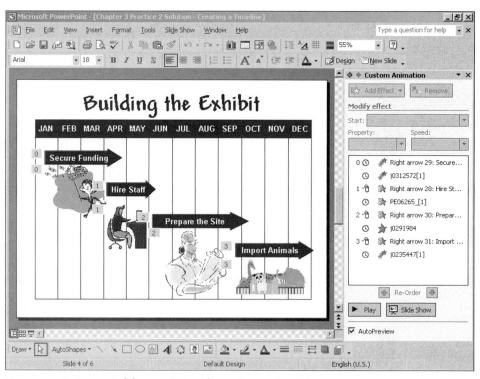

FIGURE 3.12   *Adding a Timeline (Exercise 2)*

3. Working with Photographs: The presentation in Figure 3.13 displays a collection of photographs. All of the photographs were obtained by searching the Clip Organizer within Microsoft Office. Click the button to Insert Clip Art to open the task pane, enter "Animals" as the text for your search, then restrict the results to photographs. The command works best with an active Internet connection that extends the search to the Microsoft Web site.

a. Start a new presentation. Create a title slide, and then insert a blank slide. Use the Insert Clip Art command as just described to locate multiple photographs for insertion on the slide. Arrange the pictures in an attractive overlapping fashion.

b. Select all of the photographs, then use the Format Picture command to apply a black 4-point border around every picture.

c. Check that all of the photographs are still selected. Click the Compress Photographs tool on the Picture toolbar to compress the pictures and reduce the file sizes.

d. Click on any picture to deselect all of the pictures. Pull down the Slide Show menu, click Custom Animation, and apply individual entrance effects to each of the photographs. Set each entrance so that it begins automatically after the previous animation.

e. Insert a second blank slide. Create six separate WordArt objects, each of which is a single letter, (S, A, F, A, R, and I), and each of which uses a different photograph for fill. (You have to save each picture as a separate file in order to use it as fill for a WordArt object.)

f. Use custom animation so that the objects appear in sequence, one after the other. Include the sound of applause in conjunction with the letter i when "Safari" is spelled out completely.

g. Print the title slide as a full slide to use as a cover sheet for the assignment. Print the presentation as an audience handout (two slides per page) for your instructor. Add a footer at the bottom of the page that includes your name.

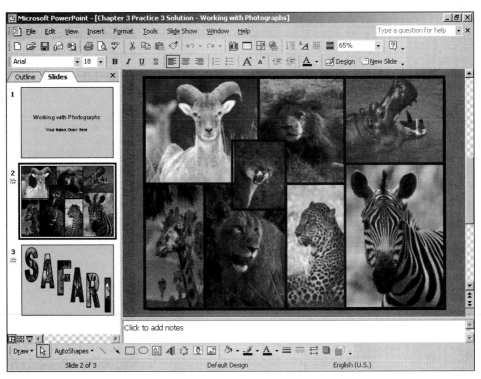

FIGURE 3.13 *Working With Photographs (Exercise 3)*

4. Organization Charts: The presentation in Figure 3.14 illustrates various ways in which to format and/or animate an organization chart. Open the partially completed presentation in *Chapter 3 Practice 4* in the Exploring PowerPoint folder and proceed as follows.

   a. Add your name to the title slide, then choose any appropriate animation for the two text objects.

   b. Go to the second slide and create an organization chart of at least four levels. Each box in the chart should contain a title and the name of an individual. Your instructor should appear at the top of the chart as the president. You should appear at the left of the second level as the first vice president. Use the default formatting.

   c. Copy the chart you just created to the remaining slides in the presentation (slides three to six). Set the formatting for each of these charts to the formatting depicted in Figure 3.14. Note, too, that in addition to changing the color and/or shape of the boxes, you are also to change the style. Slide three, for example, has left-hanging subordinates. Slide four, however, has right-hanging subordinates.

   d. Animate each chart according to the instructions that appear at the bottom of the slide. Slides two and three bring the chart in as a single object. Slides four and five, however, bring in the shapes individually, by branch and level, respectively. Slide six brings in one level at a time.

   e. Print the title slide as a full slide to use as a cover sheet for the assignment. Print the completed presentation as audience handouts (six per page) for your instructor.

   f. Do you have a better understanding of how to create and modify organization charts? Summarize your thoughts in a brief note to your instructor.

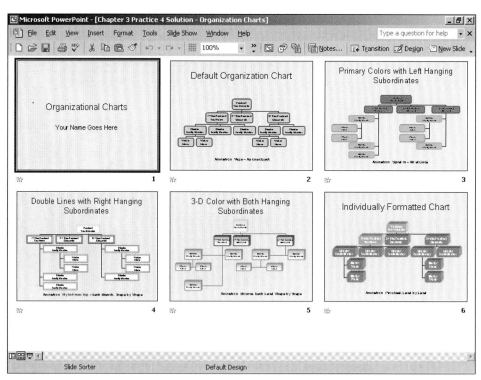

FIGURE 3.14   *Organization Charts (Exercise 4)*

5. The Diagram Gallery: Create a six slide presentation that is similar to the one in Figure 3.15. You do not have to match our presentation exactly, but you are required to include all of the indicated shapes. (The presentation includes all diagram types except for the organization chart.)

a. Start a new presentation. The title slide includes the title, "The Diagram Gallery", and your name.

b. The cycle diagram in slide two depicts the relationship between faculty, residential assistants (RAs) and administration. The goals of all three groups are to build community, promote personal growth, and support academic success.

c. The target diagram illustrates fund raising goals and associated milestones. The outer circle has a goal of $250,000 by February 1st. Each successive (smaller) circle has a higher goal in a subsequent month.

d. The pyramid diagram illustrates Maslow's hierarchy of needs. Use your favorite search engine to locate the five levels of the hierarchy if you are unable to read the text in our figure.

e. The Venn diagram illustrates a probability calculation.

f. The radial diagram depicts a simple computer network. Clip art has been placed on top of each circle in the diagram.

g. Use auto formatting and/or custom formatting to make your presentation more attractive. Add animation to each diagram as you see fit.

h. Copy the completed diagrams to the title slide, then move and size each diagram as shown in our figure.

i. Print the title slide as a full slide to use as a cover sheet for the assignment. Print the completed presentation as audience handouts (six per page) for your instructor.

j. Do you have a better understanding of the Diagram Gallery? Which type of diagram(s) will be most useful to you? Summarize your thoughts in a brief note to your instructor.

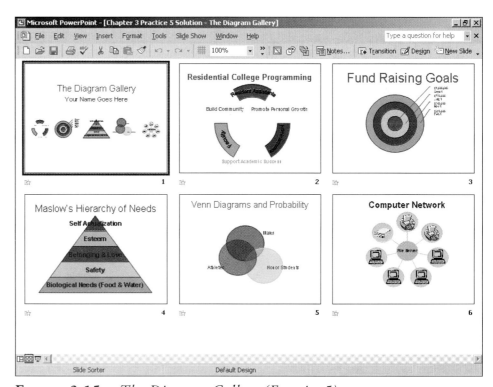

FIGURE 3.15   *The Diagram Gallery (Exercise 5)*

6. Charts and Animation Effects: The charts in Figure 3.16 are based on the data in an Excel worksheet. We want to animate the charts by individual series and category, however, and thus you have to create the charts in Microsoft Graph, as opposed to importing charts from Excel. You can, however, import the worksheet on which the charts are based. Open the partially completed presentation in *Chapter 3 Practice 6* in the Exploring PowerPoint folder and proceed as follows:

a. Add your name to the title slide. The font color for both the title and your name is black. Animate both objects to change to red automatically at the beginning of the slide show. (Use the Change Font Color effect.)

b. Select the second slide. Use the Insert Object command to insert the worksheet from the *Chapter 3 Practice 6 Excel workbook* that is found in the Exploring PowerPoint folder. Increase the size of the worksheet as shown in Figure 3.16. Use the Pinwheel animation effect for both the title and the worksheet.

c. Select the third slide and start Microsoft Graph to create the chart. Click in the upper-left area of the datasheet (the cell above row 1 and to the left of column A) to select the entire datasheet, then click the Import Data button on the Microsoft Graph toolbar to display the Import Data dialog box. Select the *Chapter 3 Practice 6 Excel workbook* (There is only one worksheet in the workbook, and you should import the entire worksheet.)

d. Move and size the chart so that it approximates the slide in Figure 3.16. Change the color of the Appetizers and Beverage series to red and yellow, respectively.

e. Copy the chart that you just created to slides four, five, and six. Modify each chart individually to match those in Figure 3.16. Add animation to the individual charts as you see fit.

f. Print the title slide as a full slide to use as a cover sheet for the assignment. Print the completed presentation as audience handouts (six per page) for your instructor.

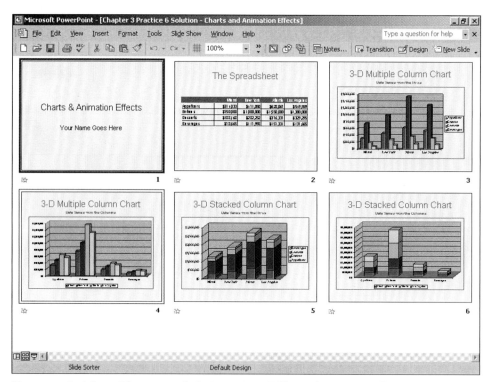

FIGURE 3.16 *Charts and Animation Effects (Exercise 6)*

7. Left Brain/Right Brain Conflict: The presentation in Figure 3.17 describes the different modes of thinking in the left and right sides of the brain. The left brain is the logical part and controls speech, language, and mathematical reasoning. The right brain is the creative part and thinks in images, colors, and remembers music and complex pictures. Open the partially completed presentation in *Chapter 3 Practice 7* and proceed as follows:

a. Add your name to the title slide, then animate the slide as you see fit.

b. The three yellow rectangles on slide two are intended to emphasize the text behind each rectangle during the presentation. Select all three rectangles and add the Dissolve In entrance effect at slow speed. The first rectangle should start on a mouse click; the next two rectangles should dissolve after the previous animation.

c. Animate slide three so that the left and right sides of the brain fly in at medium speed, from the appropriate sides of the slide, on successive mouse clicks. Each column of bulleted text should appear one item at a time as the brain appears on the slide.

d. There is no animation for slide four. Read the text of this slide carefully, however, because it represents the essence of the presentation. The slide does not contain a typo; i.e., the word "blue" appears in red letters. Your right brain tries to say the color (red), but your left brain insists on reading the word (blue).

e. Animate the words on the fifth slide so that they appear automatically, without having to click the mouse. Vary the speed at which the words appear; e.g., the first word can appear slowly, the next few at medium speed, then fast, then very fast. Test yourself to see if you can say the written color.

f. Print the completed presentation as audience handouts (six per page).

g. Nothing is required on the last side, which contains two hyperlinks to Web sites that provide additional information. Visit both sites and print a page from each site for your instructor. Submit these pages with the printout of your presentation.

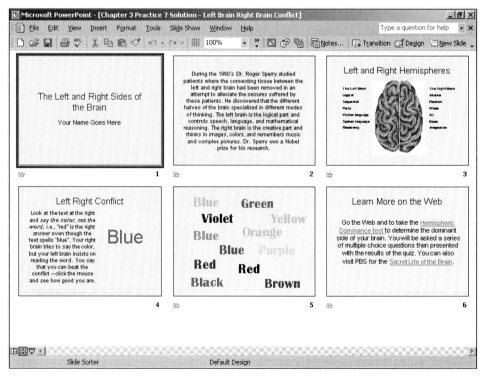

FIGURE 3.17 *Left Brain/Right Brain Conflict (Exercise 7)*

8. **The Grand Finale:** The presentation in Figure 3.18 shows you how to end a presentation with flair. You do not have to duplicate our fireworks exactly, but you are to retain the equivalent functionality. Start a new presentation and enter "The Grand Finale" as its title. Add your name to the title slide. (The title slide is there only to identify the presentation to your instructor when you submit the assignment.)

   a. Add a blank slide after the title and proceed as follows to create the fireworks. Draw and animate a curved (freeform) line to start the show. Sound and motion are important. We used Wipe from bottom as the entrance effect, at a very fast speed, to the sound of a laser. The intent is to represent a flare as it might appear during an actual fireworks display.

   b. Use the AutoShape button to create a series of large 24-point stars that appear one after another to the sound of an explosion. These large bursts are followed by a series of five-point stars that appear to the sound of a chime. The speed of these smaller stars has been manually adjusted to one tenth of a second to create a more realistic effect. (Very fast is only five tenths of a second.)

   c. Use WordArt to create the text. (You may want to use a font color other than white initially, to make it easier to see the object on the slide.) The WordArt should appear automatically when the slide is first displayed. We chose the Dissolve In entrance effect at medium speed. Now, add a second effect to increase the size of the WordArt by 25% to the sound of applause, and then add a faded zoom as an exit effect. All three effects should execute automatically, one after another at medium speed.

   d. The entire presentation should then fade to black. We found the easiest way to do this was to create a black rectangle that extended beyond the slide (use the Order command to move the rectangle to the back of the slide, so that you can see the other objects.) The rectangle should simply appear after the previous effect.

   e. Print the title slide as a full slide to use as a cover sheet for the assignment. Save the completed presentation. Print the audience handouts of the revised presentation (two slides in all) for your instructor.

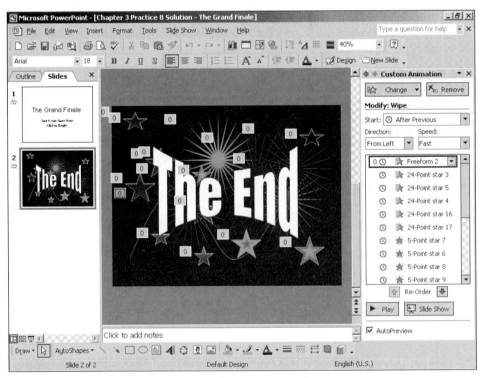

FIGURE 3.18 *The Grand Finale (Exercise 8)*

Digital Cameras

As with all technology, the price of a digital camera has come down significantly while performance has gone up dramatically. What are the most significant capabilities in a digital camera? What is the least amount of money you have to spend in order to purchase (what you consider) a worthwhile camera? What are the parameters and cost of your ideal camera? Be sure to consider the size and weight of the camera—the more functionality, the larger the camera. The worst picture is the one you do not take because the camera is too big to take with you.

Microsoft Photo Editor

You have just purchased your first digital camera and are very excited about the potential of digital photography. Your first pictures, however, are not as good as you like. There is too much background, the subject is off center, there is too much (or too little) light, and so on. Which editing programs (if any) are installed on your computer? What basic capabilities are common to these programs? Summarize your findings in a short note to your instructor.

Microsoft Producer

An "add-on" is a supplemental program that extends the capabilities of Microsoft Office by adding custom commands and specialized features. Microsoft Producer is a PowerPoint add-on that makes it easy to capture, synchronize, and publish audio, video, slides, and images. Where do you obtain the Microsoft Producer add-on and how much does it cost? How is it installed? How easy is it to use? Try to obtain a copy in order to experiment with the program, then summarize your findings in a short note to your instructor.

Microsoft Excel versus Microsoft Graph

An Excel chart can be imported into a PowerPoint presentation, and/or a chart can be created from scratch within the presentation using Microsoft Graph. Which technique is easier? Can either type of chart be linked or embedded into the presentation? What capabilities (if any) are present in Microsoft Graph, but not in the charting component of Microsoft Excel?

Movies and Video

Use the Search command on your computer to locate any movie or video files that may exist. It's easiest in Windows XP because you can specify "video," as opposed to a specific file type. How large are these files compared to documents created by other programs? Which program is required to play the video files you find? What is the Windows Movie Maker program? What features does it have, and how does it compare to similar offerings by other vendors? Summarize your findings in a short note to your instructor for class discussion.

CHAPTER 4

Advanced Techniques: Sound, Masters, Web Pages, and Broadcasting

OBJECTIVES

AFTER READING THIS CHAPTER YOU WILL BE ABLE TO:

1. Distinguish between a template and a color scheme; explain how to change and/or customize a color scheme.
2. Explain the role of masters in formatting a presentation; modify the slide master to include action buttons for easy navigation.
3. Use the Sound Recorder accessory to record a new sound, then insert that sound into a presentation.
4. Insert two hyperlinks into a presentation; one that branches to a specific slide and one that branches to an external Web site.
5. Save a PowerPoint presentation as a Web document.
6. Use the Record Narration command to add narration to a presentation; describe at least two options associated with this command.
7. Create a custom slide show; explain the advantage of having multiple custom shows within one presentation.
8. Record a Web broadcast for online delivery; distinguish between a broadcast and an online meeting.

OVERVIEW

This chapter presents several advanced features through multiple presentations in which sound is used extensively. We also show you how to make subtle changes in the appearance of a presentation by changing its color scheme. Action buttons are presented to facilitate navigation to specific slides within the presentation. We introduce the slide master, which enables you to add a common element to every slide, without having to modify the slides individually. The chapter also presents alternate means of delivery by converting a PowerPoint presentation to a series of HTML documents for distribution on a Web server and/or delivery through a Web broadcast.

177

Figure 4.1 displays a six-slide presentation in the form of a quiz. Sound is used throughout the presentation although you cannot hear anything by merely looking at our figure. Look closely, however, and you will see a Sound icon next to each potential answer in slides four and five. Click any of these icons and you will hear whether or not you are correct. A sound file is also embedded on the third slide in the form of a reminder to test the speakers and adjust the volume. Custom animation has been added to this slide, so that clicking the clip art (the icon is hidden behind the image of the speakers) will play an appropriate sound.

The use of sound requires additional hardware, namely a sound card, speakers, and a microphone if you want to record your own sound files. Multiple sound files are supplied, however, within Microsoft Windows as well as Microsoft Office. Additional sounds may be imported from the Web and/or created through the *Sound Recorder*, a Windows accessory, which creates a digitized recording of an actual sound.

The Sound Recorder uses a chip in the sound card on your computer to convert the recorded sound into a file, and then stores the file on disk. You can record any type of sound such as your voice to narrate a presentation and/or special effects such as the sound of applause. Sound files are stored just like any other type of file and can be moved and copied from one folder to another. The size of a sound file is directly proportional to its duration.

The Crayons template in Figure 4.1 may look familiar, but we have changed the underlying color scheme. A *template* controls every aspect of a presentation's design such as the background, fonts and formatting, and the size and placement of bullets and other elements. Each template has a default *color scheme*, consisting of eight balanced colors that are used for the background, text, slide title, shadows, and other accents. Change the template and you change every aspect of a presentation. Change the color scheme within a template (every template has several alternate color schemes from which to choose) and you retain the overall look, but affect a subtle change in the appearance.

Most presentations are designed for sequential viewing, starting with the first slide and ending with the last. You can also build flexibility into a presentation by including *action buttons* that will take you through the slides in a different sequence. Thus, each slide in Figure 4.1, except the title slide, contains a uniform set of four buttons to move to the first, previous, next, and last slides, respectively. You are under no obligation to use the action buttons, and indeed, you can still move through the presentation sequentially by clicking the left mouse button (or pressing the PgDn key) to move to the next sequential slide. Nevertheless, action buttons (or navigation buttons as they are sometimes called) provide a convenient way to return to the previous slide and/or jump to the last slide, which in this example contains the answer key.

The answer key on the last slide contains three *hyperlinks*, two of which return to earlier slides that contain questions one and two, and a third branches to an external link (www.prenhall.com/grauer). All three hyperlinks are created through the *Insert Hyperlink command*. Hyperlinks, like action buttons, provide flexibility for the speaker; e.g., in reviewing the answers, you can click the hyperlink to return to the associated question. You do not have to use the hyperlinks during the presentation, but the more effective public speakers are sensitive to their audience, anticipate potential questions, and take advantage of this flexibility.

Hidden slides provide additional flexibility during delivery in that they do not appear during a regular slide show. The answer key, for example, is hidden, which means that the presenter has to take explicit action to display that slide, such as clicking the appropriate action button. The hidden slide can also be displayed through the *Slide Navigator*, a tool that enables the presenter to go directly to any slide within the presentation.

(a) Title Slide

(b) Test Your Speakers

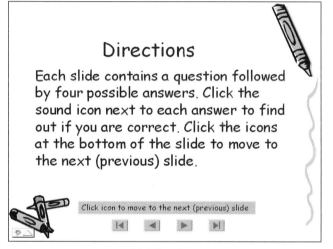

(c) Directions

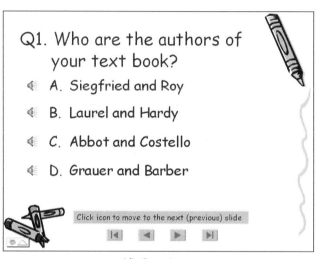

(d) Question 1

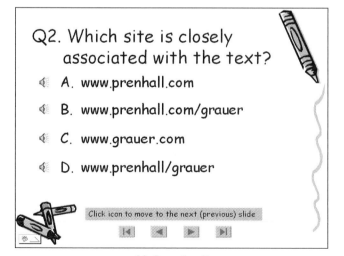

(e) Question 2

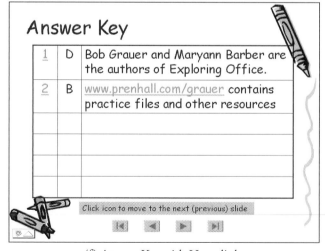

(f) Answer Key with Hyperlinks

FIGURE 4.1 *An Online Quiz*

The Slide Master

The action buttons in our presentation can be added individually to every slide, but that would be unnecessarily tedious. It is much more efficient to add the buttons to the *slide master*, as opposed to the individual slides shown in Figure 4.2. The slide master stores information about the template, including font styles, placeholder sizes and positions, background design, additional clip art or other elements, and color schemes.

The slide master is the easiest way to make global changes to a presentation. Any change to any element on the slide master is automatically reflected in every existing slide (except the title slide) as well as any new slides that are subsequently added. The title slide has its own master (as seen in Figure 4.2), although it is just as easy to make changes to the title slide itself. Additional masters are available for handouts and speaker notes.

The slide master contains a placeholder for the title of the slide, a second placeholder for the bulleted text, and additional placeholders at the bottom of the slide for the date, footer, and slide number. Change the position of any of these elements on the slide master, and the corresponding element will be changed throughout the presentation. In similar fashion, any change to the font, point size, or alignment within a placeholder also carries through to all of the individual slides.

The slide master is modified by using commands from the appropriate menu or from a toolbar. The action buttons, for example, were created through the Action Buttons command in the Slide Show menu. Clip art, such as a corporate logo, can also be added. Once the objects have been created, they can be moved and sized like any other Windows object. And, as indicated, every slide in the presentation will contain the objects that appear on the slide master. It's easy and powerful, and as you might have guessed, it is time for our first hands-on exercise.

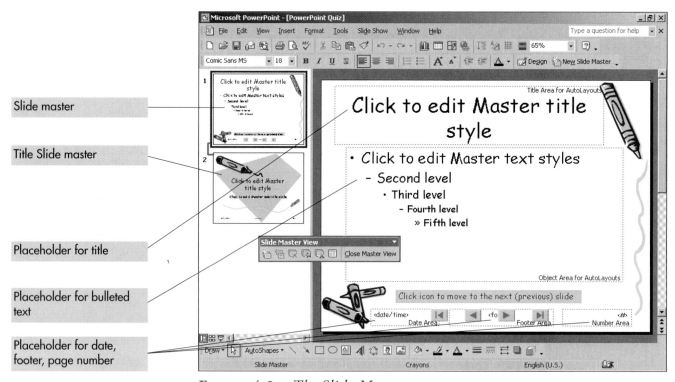

FIGURE 4.2   *The Slide Master*

INTRODUCTION TO COLOR SCHEMES, SOUND, AND THE SLIDE MASTER

Objective   To change a color scheme; to record a sound, then insert the sound onto a slide; to use the slide master to add action buttons to every slide.

Step 1:   **Change the Color Scheme**

> ➤ Open the **PowerPoint Quiz presentation** in the Exploring PowerPoint folder. Add your name to the title slide. Save the presentation as **PowerPoint Quiz Solution** so that you can return to the original presentation if necessary.
> ➤ Click the **Slide Design button** to open the task pane, then click the link to **Color Schemes** to display the color schemes for the selected design.
> ➤ Click the **down arrow** next to the second color scheme, then click the **Apply to All Slides** as shown in Figure 4.3a. The accent color on the title slide changes to light purple (the background remains white).
> ➤ Close the task pane.

Slide Design button

Click link to color schemes

Click Apply to All Slides

Click down arrow

Slide Show button

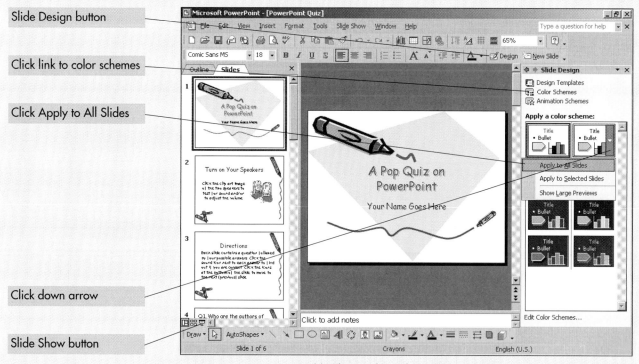

(a) Change the Color Scheme (step 1)

FIGURE 4.3   *Hands-on Exercise 1*

ADD A FAVORITE

Select the desired folder in the Open or Save As dialog boxes, click the down arrow next to the Tools button, and click the Add to Favorites command. The next time you open either dialog box you will be able to click the Favorites icon at the left of the box to go directly to the folder, as opposed to having to select the folder from the Look in list box.

Step 2: **Record the Sound(s)**

➤ Skip this step if you do not have a microphone to record your own sounds.
➤ Click the **Start button** on the Windows taskbar. Click **All Programs**, click **Accessories**, click **Entertainment**, then click **Sound Recorder** to display the associated dialog box in Figure 4.3b.
➤ Click the **red dot** to begin recording, be sure you speak directly into the microphone, and say the word "Incorrect". Click the **Stop button**.
➤ Click the **Rewind button**, then click the **Play button** to listen to the sound. If you are not satisfied, pull down the **File** menu, click **New**, then click **No** when asked whether to save the file.
➤ Pull down the **File menu** (in the Sound Recorder window) and save the file as **Incorrect** in the **Exploring PowerPoint folder**. You should see a message that the file already exists (we created a default file) and asking if you want to replace it. Click **Yes**.
➤ Record two additional files, **Sorry** and **Try Again**, in similar fashion. Close the Sound Recorder.

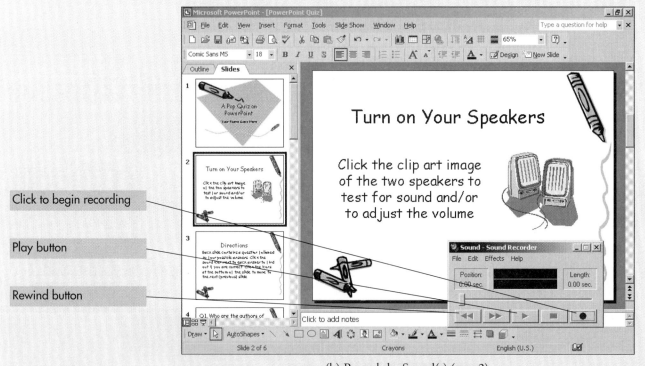

Click to begin recording

Play button

Rewind button

(b) Record the Sound(s) (step 2)

FIGURE 4.3 *Hands-on Exercise 1 (continued)*

YOU DON'T NEED STEREO

A voice can generally be converted to a lesser-quality (smaller) file, without an appreciable difference in quality. Open the Sound Recorder, pull down the File menu and click the Properties command to view the existing parameters. Click the down arrow in the Choose From list box, choose All Formats, and click the Convert Now button. Select 11kHz, 8 bit, Mono, which requires 10K bytes per second. Other settings can require as much as 180K bytes per second.

Step 3: **Insert the Sound**

➤ Select the fourth slide (the slide containing the first question in our quiz). The Sound icon does not yet appear next to the answer, "Siegfried and Roy". Pull down the **Insert menu**, click **Movies and Sounds**, then click **Sound from File** to display the Insert Sound dialog box.

➤ Change to the **Exploring PowerPoint folder**, then select the **Incorrect** sound you recorded earlier.

➤ Click the **OK button** (not visible in the figure) to insert the sound. Click **No** when asked if you want the sound to play automatically. A Sound icon should appear in the middle of the slide. Click and drag the **Sound icon** to the left of the first answer as shown in Figure 4.3c.

➤ Insert the **Try Again**, **Sorry**, and **Applause** sound files in similar fashion so that the associated Sound icons appear next to answers (b), (c), and (d), respectively. Click **No** when asked if you want the sound to play automatically.

➤ Press and hold the **Ctrl key** as you select all four **Sound icons**. Pull down the **Format menu**, click **Picture** to display the Format Picture dialog box, then click the **Position tab**. Enter **.75″** in the Horizontal list box. Click **OK**.

➤ Save the presentation.

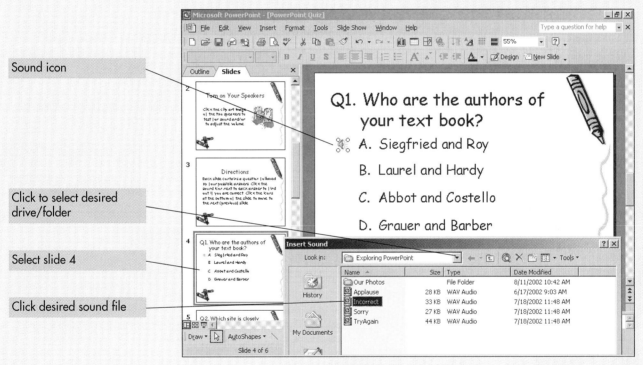

(c) Insert the Sound (step 3)

FIGURE 4.3 *Hands-on Exercise 1 (continued)*

DISCONNECT YOUR MICROPHONE

The speech recognition capabilities in Microsoft Office are quite impressive. There is a downside, however, in that a microphone will often mistake ambient noise for Office commands. You can tell this is happening if menus appear for no reason and/or random characters are continually inserted into a document. Disconnect the microphone, and the problem should disappear.

Step 4:   **Check the Answers**

➤ Select the fifth slide (the slide containing the second question in our quiz) and insert an appropriate sound file next to each answer. (The correct answer is (B), **www.prenhall.com/grauer**.) All of the sound files should be in the Exploring PowerPoint folder.

➤ Position the icons .75″ from the left border as in the previous step.

➤ Pull down the **Slide Show menu** and click the **Custom Animation command** to open the animation task pane as shown in Figure 4.3d. You should see a trigger next to each animation effect, although the number next to each sound object may be different from ours.

➤ Click the **Slide Show button** to test the slide. Click the **Sound icon** next to each answer to test the presentation. You can click each icon as often as you like. (You advance to the next slide when you click a blank space on the slide, as opposed to clicking a Sound icon.)

➤ Press **Esc** when you are satisfied the slide is correct. Close the task pane. Save the presentation.

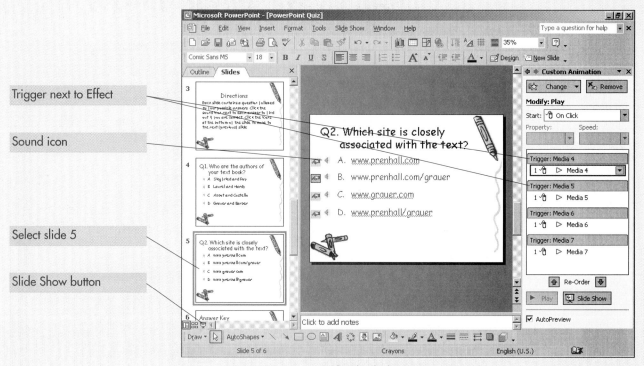

(d) Check the Answers (step 4)

FIGURE 4.3   *Hands-on Exercise 1 (continued)*

TRIGGERING A SOUND EFFECT

An animation or sound effect can be "triggered" to play in conjunction with clicking a specific object; e.g., clicking the clip art image of the microphone plays the associated sound. This differs from simply starting the effect on a mouse click, because you can click the trigger object repeatedly to play the sound as many times as you like. This technique is also used on slide two, where the sound is triggered by clicking the clip art image of the speakers.

Step 5:   **Add the Action Buttons**

➤ Pull down the **View menu**, click the **Master command**, then select the **Slide Master** to display the view in Figure 4.3e. Be sure the bulleted slide is selected, as opposed to the title slide.

➤ Pull down the **Slide Show menu**, click the **Action buttons command**, and select (click) the beginning |◄ **button** that indicates the first slide. The mouse pointer changes to a tiny crosshair.

➤ Click in the footer area at the bottom of the slide, then drag the mouse to create an action button. Release the mouse. The Action Settings dialog box is displayed automatically.

➤ The **Hyperlink to Option** button is selected and the First Slide is specified in the associated list box. Click **OK** to accept the default settings and close the Action Settings dialog box.

➤ Repeat this process three additional times to create action buttons for the previous, next, and ending slides in that sequence. Do not be concerned about the precise size or location of the buttons at this time. Save the presentation.

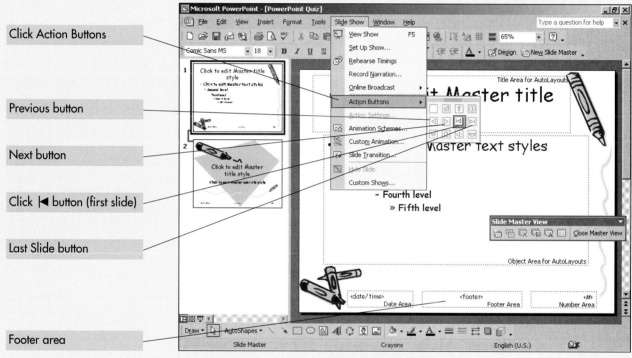

(e) Add the Action Buttons (step 5)

FIGURE 4.3   *Hands-on Exercise 1 (continued)*

THE HEADER AND FOOTER COMMAND

The Header and Footer command provides another way to display information on every slide. Pull down the View menu, click the Header and Footer command, then enter the date of the presentation, a descriptive footer, and/or the slide number in the associated dialog box. Click the Apply to All button to display these fields on every slide (or check the box to suppress the information on the title slide). The contents of these fields do not appear directly on the slide master, but are hidden within the <date/time>, <footer>, <#> fields that appear in the footer area.

Step 6: **Size and Align the Action Buttons**

➤ Click and drag the individual action buttons so that there is sufficient space between the buttons to increase their size to ½ inch each. Press and hold the **Shift key** as you click each action button to select all four buttons.

➤ Point to any button, click the **right mouse button** to display a context-sensitive menu, then click **Format AutoShape** to display the Format AutoShape dialog box.

➤ Click the **Size tab**, then enter **.35** and **.5** as the height and width of each button. Click **OK** to accept the settings and close the dialog box.

➤ Click the **Draw button** on the Drawing toolbar, select the **Align or Distribute command**, then click **Align Top** to align the buttons.

➤ Click the **Draw button** a second time, select the **Align or Distribute command**, then click **Distribute Horizontally** to allocate a uniform amount of space between each button.

➤ Add a **text box** above the action buttons as shown in Figure 4.3f. Change the fill color to match the color of the buttons.

➤ Close the Slide Master View toolbar. Save the presentation.

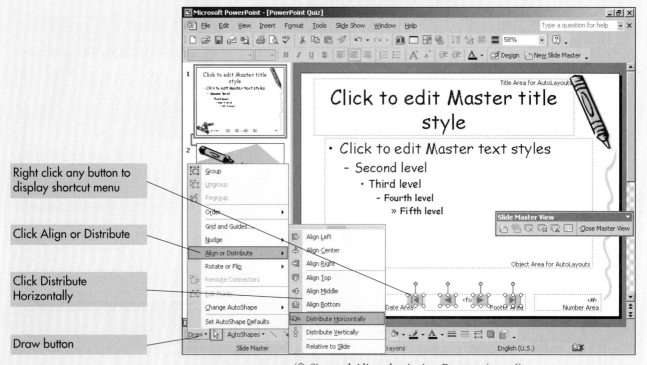

Right click any button to display shortcut menu

Click Align or Distribute

Click Distribute Horizontally

Draw button

(f) Size and Align the Action Buttons (step 6)

FIGURE 4.3 *Hands-on Exercise 1 (continued)*

MULTIPLE SLIDE MASTERS ARE POSSIBLE

Most presentations use only a single template, but there are occasions when you want to include multiple designs in the same presentation. Change to the Slide Sorter view, then press and hold the Ctrl key to select the slides that will reflect the alternate template. Click the Slide Design button on the Slide Sorter toolbar to open the task pane, click the down arrow next to the desired design, then apply the design to the selected slide(s). Repeat the process to include another design. See problem 4 at the end of the chapter.

Step 7:   **Create the Hyperlinks**

➤ Press **Ctrl+End** to move to the last slide in the presentation. The action buttons appear at the bottom of the slide because you modified the master slide layout in the previous step.

➤ Click and drag to select the number **1** in the first cell of the table, then click the **Insert Hyperlink button** on the Standard toolbar to display the associated dialog box. Click the **Place in This Document icon** and select the slide containing the first question as shown in Figure 4.3g. Click **OK**.

➤ The number 1 has been converted to a hyperlink. Create a hyperlink to the second question in similar fashion.

➤ Click and drag to select the text **www.prenhall.com/grauer** (which appears as a partial explanation for the second question). Press **Ctrl+C** to copy this link to the Windows clipboard.

➤ Click the **Insert Hyperlink button**, click the icon for **Existing file or Web page**, click in the Address text box, then press **Ctrl+V** to enter actual address. Click **OK** to create the hyperlink. Save the presentation.

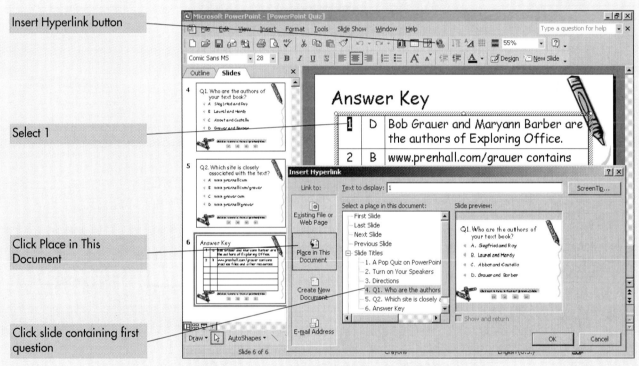

(g) Create the Hyperlinks (step 7)

FIGURE 4.3   *Hands-on Exercise 1 (continued)*

THE TABLES AND BORDERS TOOLBAR

Click anywhere within a table to display the Tables and Borders toolbar, then point to any button to display a ToolTip that is indicative of the underlying function. You can align text vertically within a cell, change the line style or thickness, distribute rows and columns evenly within a table, merge or split cells, or add a fill color. Click the down arrow next to the Table command for additional commands to insert or delete rows and columns. The tools and conventions are identical to those in Microsoft Word.

Step 8:   **Hide the Answer Key**

➤ Change to the **Slide Sorter view**. You should see three hyperlinks on the last slide, one link to each question within the presentation and one link to the Grauer Web site at www.prenhall.com/grauer.

➤ Select the last slide. Click the **Hide Slide button** on the Slide Sorter toolbar. The slide will be hidden during the slide show as can be seen from the Hidden Slide icon over the slide number below the slide.

➤ The **Hide Slide command** functions as a toggle switch. Click the button, and the slide is marked to be hidden during the presentation. Click the button a second time, and the slide is marked as visible. Set the button to hide the last slide.

➤ Check that the last slide is still selected, then click the **Transition button** on the Slide Sorter toolbar to open the task pane. Select a transition effect, a transition speed, and optionally a sound. A Transition icon appears below the slide.

➤ Save the presentation.

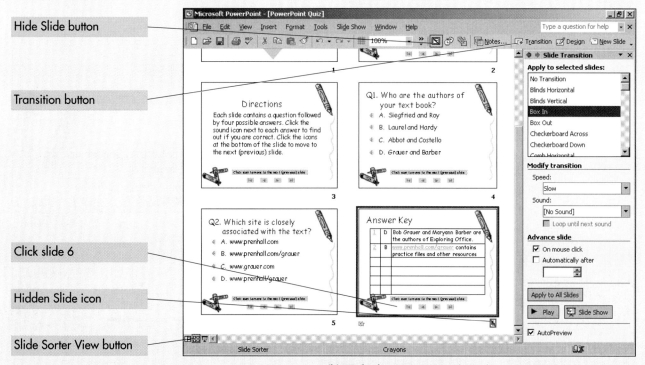

(h) Hide the Answer Key (step i)

FIGURE 4.3   *Hands-on Exercise 1 (continued)*

DISPLAY THE HIDDEN SLIDE

A hidden slide does not appear during a regular slide show, but it can be displayed at any time using the Slide Navigator. Right click any slide during a presentation, click the Go command, then click Slide Navigator to display a list of every slide. Double click any slide (parentheses appear around the number of a hidden slide) to display that slide, and then continue with the presentation from that point.

Step 9:   **Take the Quiz**

➤ Press **Ctrl+Home** to move to the first slide in the presentation. Pull down the **Slide Show menu** and click the **View Show command**.
   • You should see the title slide. Click the mouse or press the **PgDn key** to move to the second slide.
   • Click the icon to test the speakers. Move to the next slide.
   • Read the directions. Click the **action button** to move to the next slide.
   • You should see the first question as shown in Figure 4.3i. Click the **Sound icon** next to each answer. Move to the next slide.
   • Click the **Sound icon** next to each answer. Click a blank area to move to the next slide. You do not see the answer key because the slide is hidden.
➤ Press **Esc** to return to PowerPoint. Print audience handouts (six per page) for your instructor. Exit PowerPoint if you do not want to continue with the next exercise at this time.

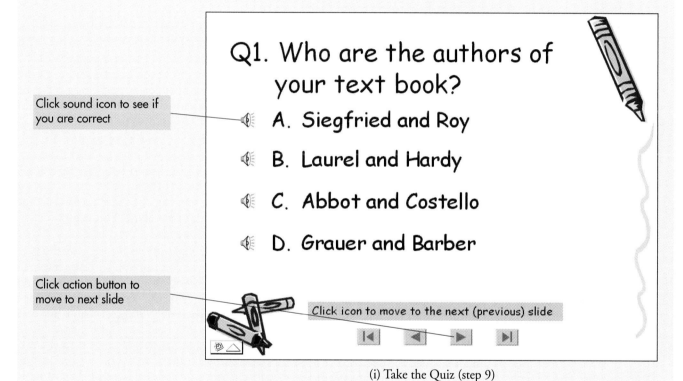

(i) Take the Quiz (step 9)

FIGURE 4.3   *Hands-on Exercise 1 (continued)*

KEYBOARD SHORTCUTS DURING THE SLIDE SHOW

Use the keyboard to gain additional flexibility during a slide show. Press the letter B to toggle between a black screen and the slide show (or the letter W to toggle between a White screen and the slide show). Type a number plus the enter key to go to a specific slide or press the letter H plus the enter key to display the next hidden slide. Use Ctrl+P to change the mouse pointer to a pen to annotate the slide, then press E to erase the annotations. Press Ctrl+A to change the mouse pointer back to an arrow. And if you can't remember these shortcuts, press the F1 key to see the entire list of shortcuts.

Perhaps you have already created a home page and have uploaded it to the World Wide Web. If so, you know that the process is not difficult, and have experienced the satisfaction of adding your documents to the Web. If not, this is a good time to learn. This section describes how to convert a PowerPoint presentation into a series of Web pages for display on the Web or local area network.

All Web pages are written in a language called ***HTML (HyperText Markup Language)***. Initially, the only way to create a ***Web page*** was to learn HTML. Microsoft Office simplifies the process as it lets you create the document in any Office application, then simply save it as a Web page. In other words, you start PowerPoint in the usual fashion and enter the text of the presentation with basic formatting. However, instead of saving the document in the default format (as a PowerPoint presentation), you use the ***Save As Web Page command*** to convert the presentation to HTML. PowerPoint does the rest and generates the HTML statements for you. You do not have to place the resulting document on the Web, but can view it locally using an Internet browser.

Figure 4.4 displays two different views of the title slide of our next presentation. Figure 4.4a shows the expanded outline and the associated speaker notes (if any) with the selected slide. Figure 4.4b shows only the title of each slide and suppresses the details in the outline. The most significant difference, however, is the location of the presentation. Figure 4.4a displays the presentation from a local drive, whereas Figure 4.4b displays the presentation from a Web server. Viewing a Web page locally is useful for two reasons. First, it lets you test the page before uploading to the Web. Second, you can restrict access to a local area network, which is useful in a corporate setting to view documents on an "Intranet," which is limited to those within the organization.

In any event, the Internet Explorer window is divided into two vertical frames and is similar to the Normal view in PowerPoint. The left frame displays the title of each slide, and these titles function as links; that is, you can click any title in the left frame, and the corresponding slide is displayed in the right pane. You can also click and drag the border separating the panes to change the size of the panes.

The buttons above the status bar provide additional options for viewing the presentation. (The buttons were created automatically in conjunction with the Save As Web Page command when the presentation was saved initially.) The Show/Hide Outline button toggles the left (outline) pane on and off. The Expand/Collapse Outline button appears to the right of the outline when the outline is visible and lets you vary the detail of the outline. The Show/Hide Notes button toggles a notes pane on and off at the bottom of the slide. The left and right arrows move to the previous and next slide, respectively. The Slide Show button at the lower right creates a slide show on the Internet that is identical to the slide show viewed within PowerPoint.

Uploading a Presentation

Creating a Web document is only the beginning in that you may want to place the page on the Web, so that other people will be able to access it. This in turn requires you to obtain an account on a Web server, which is a computer with Internet access and adequate disk space to hold the various pages you create. You need to check with your system administrator at school or work, or with your local Internet provider, to determine how to submit your Web page when it is complete.

As indicated earlier, you can still view a Web page locally, even if you do not place it on a Web server. This is the approach we follow in the next hands-on exercise, which has you create an HTML document. Your document is stored on a local drive (e.g., on drive A or drive C) rather than on a Web server, but it can still be viewed through Internet Explorer (or any other browser). After you have completed the exercise, you (and/or your instructor) can determine if it is worthwhile to place your page on your school or university's server, where it can be accessed by anyone.

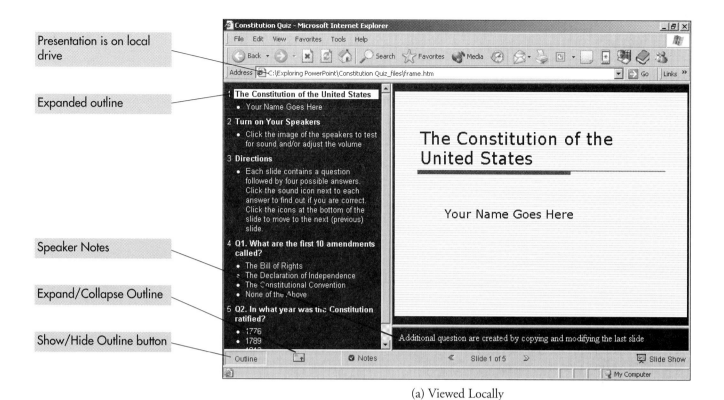

Presentation is on local drive

Expanded outline

Speaker Notes

Expand/Collapse Outline

Show/Hide Outline button

(a) Viewed Locally

Presentation is on Web

Slide Titles only

Slide Show button

Next Slide

Previous Slide

Show/Hide Notes button

(b) On a Web Server

FIGURE 4.4 *PowerPoint Web Pages*

PRESENTATIONS ON THE WEB

Objective To save a presentation as a Web page, then view the result in Internet Explorer; to modify the newly created Web document in PowerPoint.

Step 1: **Create the Web Page**

> ➤ Open the **Create a Quiz presentation** in the **Exploring PowerPoint folder**. Change the title to **The Constitution of the United States**.
> ➤ Add your name to the title slide. Click in the **Speaker Notes** area and enter the text shown in Figure 4.5a.
> ➤ Pull down the **File menu** and click the **Save As Web Page command** to display the Save as dialog box. Select the **Exploring PowerPoint folder**. Save the file as the **Constitution Quiz**. The file type should be specified as **Web Page**.
> ➤ Click the **Save button** to save the presentation as a Web page. The title bar changes to the name of the Web page (Constitution Quiz), but the display does not change in any other way.

Click down arrow to select drive/folder

Publish button provides additional options

Enter filename

Normal View button

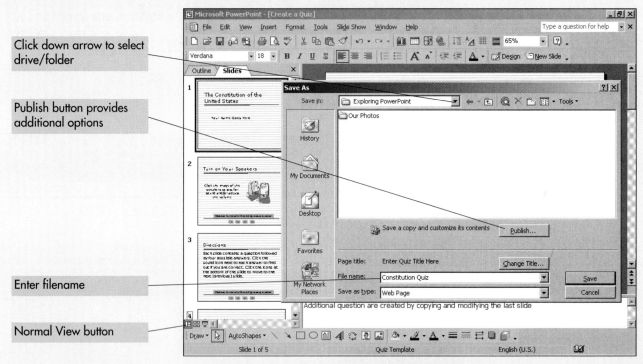

(a) Create the Web Page (step 1)

FIGURE 4.5   *Hands-on Exercise 2*

PUBLISHING OPTIONS

Click the Publish button in the Save as dialog box to display the Publish as Web page dialog box, where you view and/or modify the various options associated with an HTML document. The default publishing options work well, but you have total control over your Web pages.

Step 2: **Add the Additional Slides**

➤ The Create a Quiz Presentation, with which we began the exercise, is generic, and thus specific questions have to be added. This will be accomplished by copying the last (empty question) slide multiple times, and modifying each slide accordingly.

➤ Change to the **Slide Sorter view**. Press **Ctrl+End** to move to the last slide. Press and hold the **Ctrl key** as you drag the last slide to the left of the answer key. Release the mouse to duplicate the slide.

➤ The newly copied slide should still be selected. Click the **Hide Slide button** on the Slide Sorter toolbar to unhide this slide as shown in Figure 4.5b.

➤ Click the **Copy button** or press **Ctrl+C** to copy the new (and unhidden) slide to the clipboard. Press **Ctrl+V** to paste the copied slide into the presentation, which should now contain a total of seven slides (the original five slides plus the two you just added).

➤ Save the presentation.

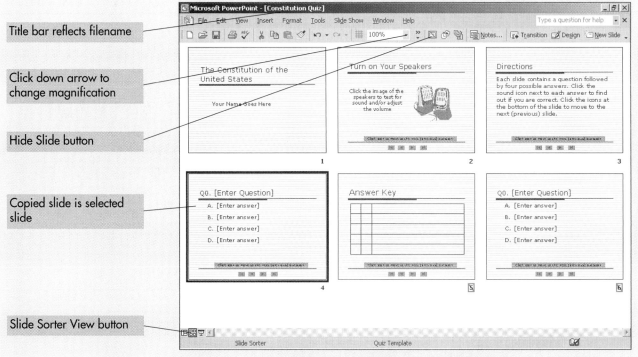

(b) Add the Additional Slides (step 2)

FIGURE 4.5 *Hands-on Exercise 2 (continued)*

CHANGE THE MAGNIFICATION

Click the down arrow on the Zoom box to change the display magnification, which in turn determines the size of individual slides. The higher the magnification, the easier it is to read the text of an individual slide, but the fewer slides you see at one time. Conversely, changing to lower magnification decreases the size of the individual slides, but enables you to see more of the presentation. You can also change the size of either pane in the Normal view in similar fashion.

Step 3: **Create the Questions**

➤ Change to the **Normal view** and select the fourth slide. Change Q0 to **Q1**. Replace the default text with the question on the first 10 amendments to the constitution as shown in Figure 4.5c.

➤ Pull down the **Insert menu**, click **Movies and Sounds**, then click **Sound from File** to display the Insert Sound dialog box. Select the **Applause** sound and click **OK.** Click **No** when asked if you want the sound to play automatically. A Sound icon should appear in the middle of the slide.

➤ Click and drag the **Sound icon** to the left of the first answer, **The Bill of Rights**, which is the correct answer. Insert the other sounds to signify an erroneous answer next to the remaining choices.

➤ Press and hold the **Ctrl key** as you select all four **Sound icons**. Pull down the **Format menu**, click **Picture** to display the Format Picture dialog box, then click the **Position tab**. Enter **.75″** in the Horizontal list box. Click **OK.**

➤ Create the second question as shown in Figure 4.5c. Insert the appropriate sound files next to each answer, placing the Applause file next to part (b). Align the sound icons **.75 inch** from the left edge of the slide.

➤ Save the presentation.

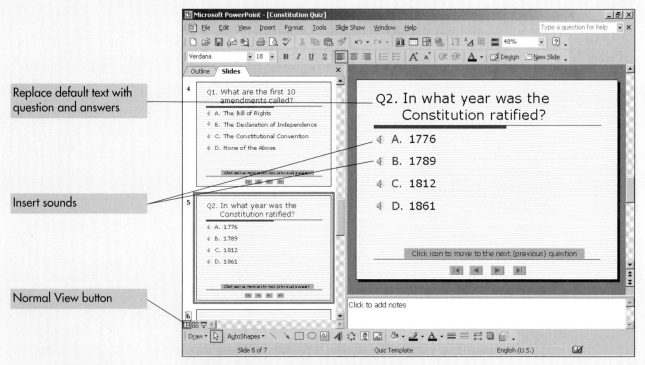

(c) Create the Questions (step 3)

FIGURE 4.5 *Hands-on Exercise 2 (continued)*

ALIGN, DISTRIBUTE, AND NUDGE

You can align the objects left, center, or right (vertical stack), or top, middle, or bottom (horizontal row). Press and hold the Ctrl key as you select multiple objects on a slide, then click the down arrow on the Draw button within the Drawing toolbar to position the selected objects. You can also create uniform space between the objects by distributing horizontally or vertically. You can even nudge the objects by moving them slightly in the desired direction.

Step 4:   **Open the Web Page**

➤ You can view the Web page you just created even if it has not been saved on a Web server. Start **Internet Explorer** if it is not already open, or click its button on the Windows taskbar.

➤ Pull down the **File menu** and click the **Open command** to display the Open dialog box in Figure 4.5d.

➤ Click the **Browse button**, then select the folder and drive (e.g., **Exploring PowerPoint** on drive C) where you saved the Web page.

➤ Select the **Constitution Quiz** and click **Open**, which closes the dialog box. The selected file has been inserted in the original Open dialog box. Click **OK** to open the presentation.

➤ You should see the presentation that was created earlier, except that you are viewing it in Internet Explorer rather than PowerPoint. The Address bar reflects the local address (in the Exploring PowerPoint folder) of the presentation.

Click Browse button

Click to select drive/folder

Select file

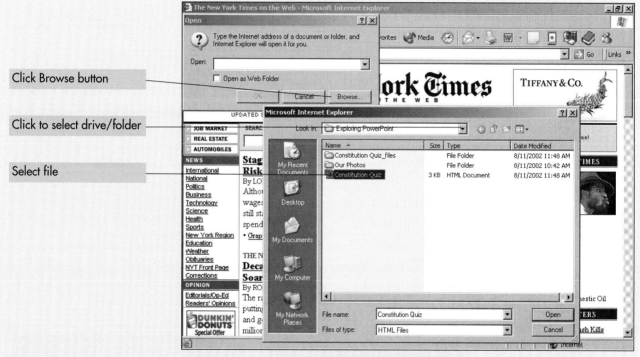

(d) Open the Web Page (step 4)

FIGURE 4.5   *Hands-on Exercise 2 (continued)*

AN EXTRA FOLDER

Look carefully at the contents of the Exploring PowerPoint folder within the Open dialog box. You see the Constitution Quiz HTML document (note the file size) that you just created, as well as a folder that was created automatically by the Save As Web page command. The latter contains the various objects that are referenced by the HTML pages within the presentation. Be sure to copy the contents of this folder to the Web server in addition to your Web page if you decide to post the page.

Step 5: **View the Presentation**

➤ Explore the navigation controls that appear at the bottom of the Internet Explorer window as shown in Figure 4.5e. (If you do not see these controls, return to step 3 and save the presentation with these controls. Click the **Publish button** in the Save as dialog box, click the **Web Options command button**, click **General**, then check the appropriate box.)

➤ Click the **Show/Hide Outline button** at the bottom left to show or hide the outline. Click the **Expand/Collapse Outline button** (when the outline is visible) to vary the detail of the outline.

➤ Click the **Notes button** to show/hide the Notes pane at the bottom of the window. The title page is the only slide that contains a note.

➤ Click the **Slide Show button** at the lower right of the Internet Explorer window to start the slide show.

➤ This is the identical slide show that you would see if you were viewing the presentation from within PowerPoint. Stop the show at any time by pressing the **Esc key** to return to the view in Figure 4.5e.

➤ Click the **Edit button** on the Standard Buttons toolbar to return to PowerPoint.

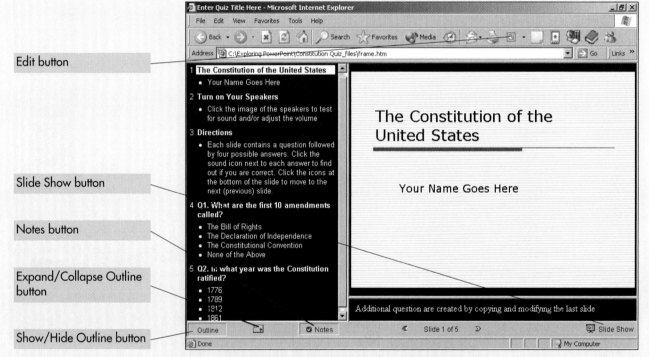

(e) View the Presentation (step 5)

FIGURE 4.5   *Hands-on Exercise 2 (continued)*

TWO WAYS TO NAVIGATE

The previous and next slide buttons within the Internet Explorer window may appear redundant with the corresponding action buttons that were added explicitly to the PowerPoint slides. Note, however, that you can click the Slide Show button within Internet Explorer to show a presentation on the Web, which in turn (temporally) closes Internet Explorer and reverts to a true PowerPoint presentation in which the action buttons are essential.

Step 6:   **Modify the Presentation**

➤ You should be back in PowerPoint. If necessary, change to the **Normal view**, and then select the sixth slide (the slide containing the answer key). Enter the answers to the first two questions as shown in Figure 4.5f.

➤ Click and drag to select the number of the first question, click the **Insert Hyperlink button** on the Standard toolbar, and set the link to slide four (the slide containing the first question). Create a hyperlink for the second question in similar fashion.

➤ Right click the slide containing the answer key to display a context-sensitive menu as shown in Figure 4.5f, then click the **Hide Slide command** to display the slide during a slide show. The icon next to the slide will change to show that the slide is no longer hidden.

➤ **Save the presentation.** This is very important, because if you do not save the presentation, these changes will not be visible when you return to Internet Explorer.

➤ Click the **Internet Explorer button** on the Windows taskbar to return to the Web presentation.

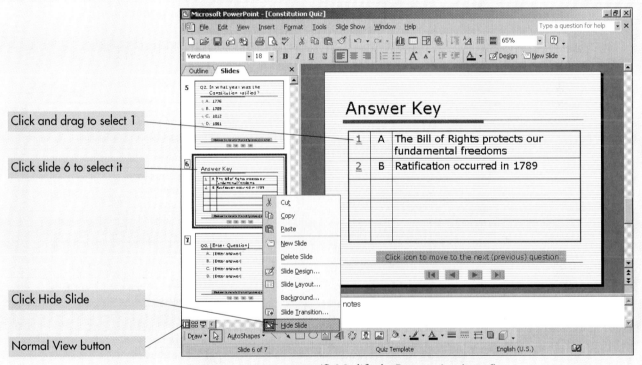

(f) Modify the Presentation (step 6)

FIGURE 4.5   *Hands-on Exercise 2 (continued)*

ROUND TRIP HTML

All applications in Microsoft Office enable you to open an HTML document in the Office application that created it. In other words, you can start with a PowerPoint presentation, use the Save As Web Page command to convert the presentation to a series of HTML documents, then view those documents in a Web browser. You can then reopen the HTML document in PowerPoint (the original Office application) and have full access to all PowerPoint commands if you want to modify the document.

Step 7: **View the Corrected Presentation**

➤ You should be back in Internet Explorer, although the answer key is not yet visible. Click the **Refresh button** on the Standard buttons toolbar to display the most recent version of your presentation.

➤ Select the **Answer key** slide in the left pane to display the associated slide in the right pane. Click the **hyperlink** to the first question to test the link. Return to the slide containing the answer key. Test the hyperlink to the second question in similar fashion.

➤ You can improve the presentation further by changing the text of the title bar (which currently says, "Enter Quiz Title Here"). Click the **Edit button** to return to PowerPoint.

➤ Pull down the **File menu** and click the **Save As Web Page command** to display the associated dialog box. Click the **Change Title button** to display the Set Page Title dialog box, enter **Constitution Quiz**, and click **OK**. Click **Save** to save the page. Click **Yes** if asked whether to replace the existing presentation.

➤ Click the **Internet Explorer button** on the Windows taskbar to return to the Web presentation, then click the **Refresh button** to see the updated presentation. The title bar should reflect the new title as shown in Figure 4.7g.

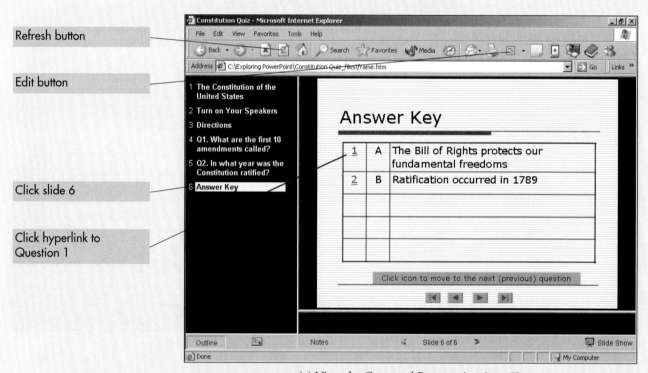

(g) View the Corrected Presentation (step 7)

FIGURE 4.5 *Hands-on Exercise 2 (continued)*

THE SAVE AS COMMAND

The Save As command saves a presentation under a different name, and is useful when you want to retain a copy of the original presentation prior to making any changes. The original (unmodified) presentation is kept on disk under its original name. A second copy of the presentation is saved under a new name and remains in memory. All subsequent editing is done on the new presentation.

Step 8:   **Print the Web Page**

➤ Select the first slide. Pull down the **File menu** (in Internet Explorer) and click the **Print Preview command** to display the screen in Figure 4.5h. If necessary, click the **down arrow** on the zoom box to adjust the magnification so that you can read the page header.

➤ Click the **Page Setup button** on the Print Preview toolbar to display the associated dialog box.

➤ Click the **question mark** (help button) in the Page Setup dialog box, then point to the header list box to see an explanation of the associated codes, then compare these codes to the appearance of the printed page. The default settings display the title and the number of pages at the top of the page.

➤ Close the Page Setup dialog box. Print the title page of the presentation for your instructor to show that you have created the Web page.

➤ Close Internet Explorer and return to PowerPoint. Print the audience handouts, six per page, to show the completed presentation.

➤ Save the presentation. Exit PowerPoint if you do not want to continue with the next exercise.

Page Setup button

Zoom box

Click question mark

Point to header box

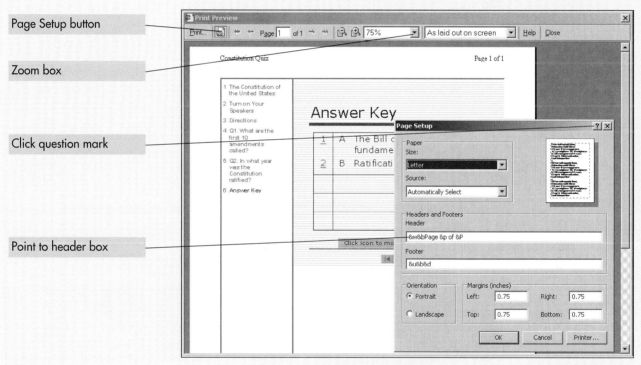

(h) Print the Web Page (step 8)

FIGURE 4.5   *Hands-on Exercise 2 (continued)*

PRINT FROM POWERPOINT

Internet Explorer is great for viewing Web pages, but less than ideal for printing them. PowerPoint provides far more flexibility. Click the Edit button on the Standard Toolbars button in Internet Explorer to return to PowerPoint, then pull down the File menu and click the Print command. You can print individual slides, audience handouts, a presentation outline, and/or speaker notes.

The presentations thus far have used limited sound, which was played on demand by the viewer. This section describes how to add narration (or voiceover) that plays automatically when a presentation is delivered. Narration is very useful to create a self-running presentation for a trade show or kiosk and/or to embellish a Web-based presentation.

Figure 4.6 displays a six-slide presentation in the Slide Sorter view that represents a hypothetical introduction to this course as it might be delivered by your professor. The **Record Narration command** creates a specific narrative (sound file) for each slide and also records the required time for that narrative. Look closely, and you will see a sound icon on each slide as well as the associated time. Once the narrative has been created, you can set the presentation to play automatically, advancing from one slide to the next, in conjunction with your voice.

We recommend that you create a script and rehearse the presentation prior to recording it, so that the narrative flows smoothly, but if necessary you can rerecord the entire presentation as often as you like. You can also delete the sound file on an individual slide, use the Windows Sound Recorder to create a new file for just that slide, and then use the Custom Animation command to substitute the new recording.

Sound files can grow very large as the duration increases, and thus you are given the choice to link or embed the narration at the time of recording. Linking creates individual sound files for each slide, which in turn decreases the size of the presentation itself. Linking makes it more difficult, however, to copy the presentation to another computer (or upload it to the Web) because you must remember to take all of the files (the presentation as well as the individual sound files). Embedding creates a larger presentation, but results in a single file. Either technique is acceptable, however, and the choice is up to you.

Our next exercise also describes how to create a **custom show**, consisting of a subset of slides within the presentation, to play for a specific audience. Multiple custom shows can be created within one presentation.

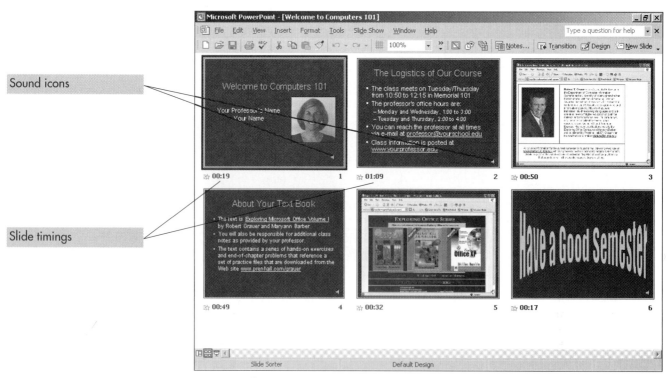

Sound icons

Slide timings

FIGURE 4.6 *Narrating a Presentation*

NARRATING A PRESENTATION

Objective   Add narration to a presentation; create a custom show within an existing presentation. Use Figure 4.7 as a guide in doing the exercise.

Step 1:   **Open the Presentation**

➤ Open the **Welcome to Computers 101** presentation in the **Exploring PowerPoint folder** as shown in Figure 4.7a. The presentation consists of six slides that describe an introductory computer course.

➤ Add **your name** and **your professor's name** to the title slide. Replace Maryann's picture with your own or with that of an instructor if a photo is available.

➤ Change the text of the second slide so that the information corresponds to the logistics of your specific course. The remaining slides can be used without any modification.

➤ Save the presentation as **Welcome to Computers 101 Solution**.

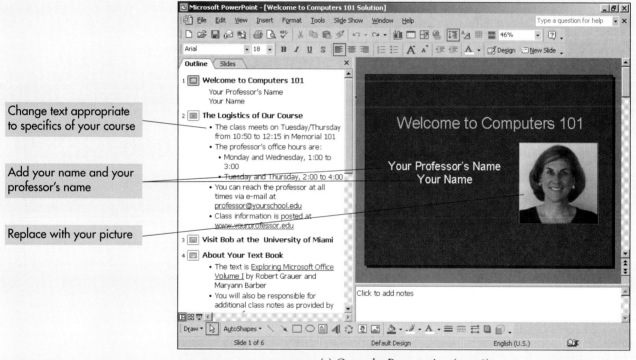

Change text appropriate to specifics of your course

Add your name and your professor's name

Replace with your picture

(a) Open the Presentation (step 1)

FIGURE 4.7   *Hands-on Exercise 3*

REHEARSE THE PRESENTATION

You should create a script and rehearse your presentation before recording so that the narrative flows smoothly. Even if you are well rehearsed, you can still make a mistake, in which case you can simply rerecord the entire presentation. You can also delete the sound file on an individual slide, then use the Windows Sound Recorder to create a new file for just that slide.

Step 2: **Record the Narration**

➤ Press **Ctrl+Home** to move to the first slide. Pull down the **Slide Show menu** and click the **Record Narration command** to display the Record Narration dialog box.

➤ Click the **Change Quality command button** to display the Sound Selection dialog box in Figure 4.7b.

➤ Click the **down arrow** in the name box and select **Telephone Quality**. Click **OK**. You do not need CD quality if you are recording a speaking voice.

➤ It's easier to embed the sound files into the presentation, as opposed to linking to individual files. Thus, the box to link narration should be clear.

➤ Click the **Set Microphone Level command button** to test the microphone. Read the text into the mike. You should see a set of green squares to indicate that the microphone is working properly. Click **OK** to close the Microphone Check dialog box.

➤ Click **OK** to begin recording your presentation. You should see the first slide in your presentation. Speak naturally and introduce yourself as the instructor.

➤ Click the mouse to move to the next slide. Continue speaking into the microphone as you move from one slide to the next. Press **Esc** when finished.

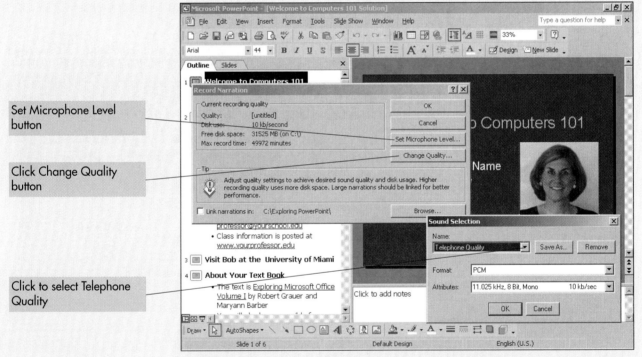

Set Microphone Level button

Click Change Quality button

Click to select Telephone Quality

(b) Record the Narration (step 2)

FIGURE 4.7 *Hands-on Exercise 3 (continued)*

CHOOSE THE APPROPRIATE OPTIONS

A two-minute voice recording will require approximately 1200 kilobytes or 1.2 megabytes of storage, given a recording rate of 10kb per second. At CD quality, however, the same recording requires almost 20 megabytes, given a recording rate of 172 kb/second, and you will be hard pressed to hear the difference. Be sure to select telephone quality prior to recording.

Step 3: **Set Up the Presentation**

> ➤ You will see a message indicating that the narrations have been saved with each slide and asking whether you want to save the slide timings as well. Click the **Save button**.
> ➤ You should see a screen similar to Figure 4.7c. The time required for each slide appears under the slide within the Slide Sorter view.
> ➤ Pull down the **Slide Show menu** and click the **Set Up Show command** to display the associated dialog box. The check boxes in the Show options area should be clear. Be sure the option to Advance slides Using timings is selected.
> ➤ Click **OK**. Select the first slide, then click the **Slide Show button** above the status bar to begin the presentation. The slides should advance automatically, and you should hear the associated narration as each slide appears on the screen.
> ➤ You can replace the narration for the entire presentation by repeating step 2 on the previous page. Alternatively, you can replace the narration (sound file) for an individual slide as described in step 4.
> ➤ Save the presentation.

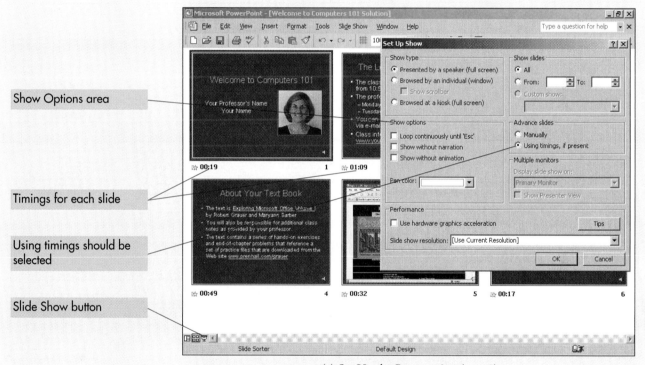

Show Options area

Timings for each slide

Using timings should be selected

Slide Show button

(c) Set Up the Presentation (step 3)

FIGURE 4.7 *Hands-on Exercise 3 (continued)*

THE REHEARSE TIMINGS COMMAND

The Record Narration command is similar in concept to the Rehearse Timings command, except that the latter does not include recorded sound. The Rehearse Timings command does, however, display a Rehearsal toolbar that lets you pause and catch your breath as you practice your speech for each slide. The Rehearsal toolbar also displays the amount of time spent on each slide as well as the total time for the presentation. Unfortunately, the toolbar is not available in conjunction with the Record Narration command.

Step 4: **Modify the Narration**

➤ Skip this step if you are satisfied with the narration for the entire presentation. Otherwise, return to the **Normal view** and select the slide where you want to replace the narration. Select the **Sound icon**.

➤ Pull down the **Slide Show menu** and open the Custom Animation task pane as shown in Figure 4.7d. Click the **Play button** to hear the narration to be sure you want to replace it. The Sound icon should still be selected. Press the **Del key**.

➤ Start the Sound Recorder, click the **red dot** to begin recording, and click the **Stop button** when you are finished. Click the **Rewind button**, then click the **Play button** to listen to the sound. Save this file in the same folder as the other sounds for this presentation. Close the Sound Recorder.

➤ Pull down the **Insert menu**, click **Movies and Sounds**, then click **Sound from File** to display the Insert Sound dialog box. Locate the new narration, click **OK**, then click **Yes** when asked if you want the sound to play automatically. Move the Sound icon to the lower-right corner of the slide.

➤ The animation task pane should show that the sound object (Media 5 on our slide) will play automatically after the previous effect; in other words, the narration plays automatically when the slide is displayed. Close the task pane.

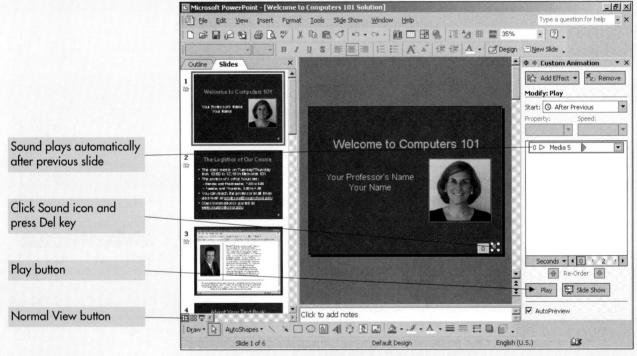

Sound plays automatically after previous slide

Click Sound icon and press Del key

Play button

Normal View button

(d) Modify the Narration (step 4)

FIGURE 4.7 *Hands-on Exercise 3 (continued)*

THE SOUND RECORDER

Click the Start button, click All Programs, click Accessories, click Entertainment, then click Sound Recorder to display the associated dialog box. Pull down the File menu, click the Properties command, and then click the Convert Now button. Select telephone quality as both the recording and playback format. Be sure to save the recorded file in the appropriate folder.

Step 5: **Create the Custom Shows**

> ➤ Pull down the **Slide Show menu** and click the **Custom Shows command** to display the Custom Shows dialog box. Click the **New button** to display the Define Custom Show dialog box in Figure 4.7e.
> ➤ Enter **Grauer on the Web** as the name of the new show. Select (click) slide number three, **Bob Grauer at the University of Miami**, then click the **Add button**. The selected slide appears in the left column as the first slide in the custom show.
> ➤ Double click slide number five, **The Grauer Web Site**, to add this slide as well. Both slides should now appear in the left column. Click **OK** to close this dialog box. The newly created show, Grauer on the Web, should appear in the Custom Shows dialog box.
> ➤ Click the **New button** to create a second custom show. Enter **Logistics and Text** as the name of the second custom show. Double click **slides two and four** to add these slides to this show. Click **OK** to create the show.
> ➤ Click the **Close button** to close the Custom Shows dialog box. Save the presentation.

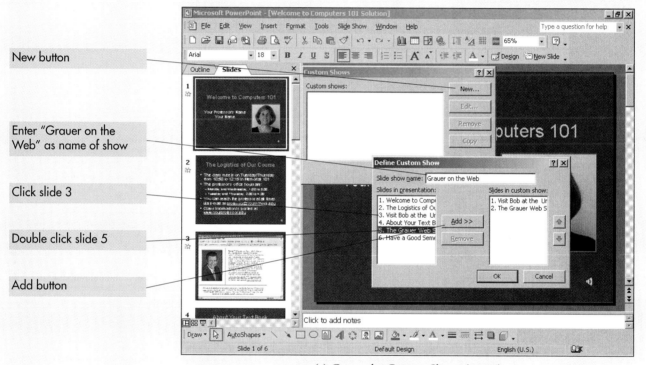

New button

Enter "Grauer on the Web" as name of show

Click slide 3

Double click slide 5

Add button

(e) Create the Custom Shows (step 5)

FIGURE 4.7 *Hands-on Exercise 3 (continued)*

DIFFERENT SHOWS FOR DIFFERENT AUDIENCES

Many presenters are faced with the task of creating nearly identical shows for different audiences. There is a "basic show" common to every audience, followed by a few special slides for each audience. You could create multiple presentations and store each presentation in its own file. It is much more efficient, however, to create custom shows within a single presentation. This saves time and effort, especially if you have to update information on a basic slide, in that you would make the change only once.

Step 6: **Show Time**

➤ Pull down the **Slide Show menu** and click the **Custom Shows command**. Select the first custom show, **Grauer on the Web**. Click the **Show button**.

➤ You should see the slide containing Bob's home page at the University of Miami as shown in Figure 4.7g. You should also hear the accompanying narration.

➤ The next slide in the custom show, The Grauer Web site, should appear automatically with its narration, after which the presentation ends. Press **Esc** to return to PowerPoint.

➤ Pull down the **Slide Show menu** to view the second custom show, **Logistics and Text**, which also contains two slides. Press the **Esc key** at the end of the show to return to PowerPoint.

➤ Exit PowerPoint if you do not want to continue with the next exercise at this time.

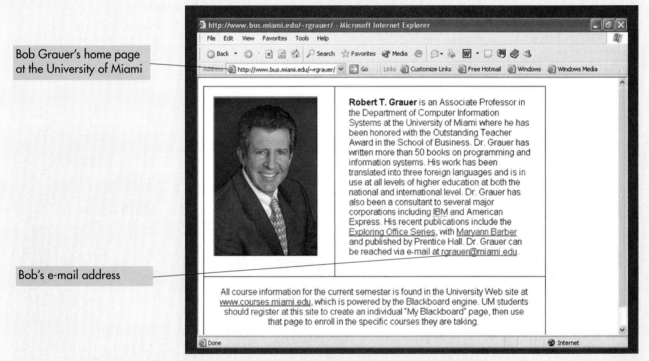

(f) Show Time (step 6)

FIGURE 4.7 *Hands-on Exercise 3 (continued)*

ADD HYPERLINKS TO YOUR CUSTOM SHOWS

Create a table of contents in the form of hyperlinks to the various custom shows in your presentation. Press Ctrl+Home to move to the title slide, insert a text box, then enter the name of each custom show on a separate line. Click and drag to select the name of the first custom show, click the Insert Hyperlink button to display the associated text box, and click the Place in this Document icon at the left. Scroll, if necessary, until you can select the appropriate custom show. Check the box to show and return, and click OK. Do this for each custom show. Click the Slide Show button, then view your custom shows from the title slide.

Any presentation, including video and audio, can be delivered as a *Web broadcast*. The broadcast can be live or recorded. A live broadcast is scheduled at a precise time, and invitations are sent to a designated list of attendees. A recorded broadcast is uploaded to a Web server and configured for on-demand viewing. Either type of broadcast is ideal for reaching large and/or geographically dispersed audiences. PowerPoint alone is sufficient to deliver a broadcast to groups of 10 individuals or less. Additional software, such as Microsoft Windows Media Server, is required to reach larger audiences.

PowerPoint also supports *online meetings* in addition to Web broadcasts. A broadcast is a one-way connection in which you speak, and the audience listens. An online meeting is a two-way connection in which everyone can communicate with everyone else. Online meetings are limited to 10 or fewer attendees and require the Microsoft NetMeeting software.

Figure 4.8 displays the opening slide in the Web broadcast that we will create in the next hands-on exercise. A Web broadcast is viewed in Internet Explorer and is similar in appearance to a presentation that is saved as a Web page. The controls for the presentation appear in the left pane. You can start and stop the presentation at will and/or adjust the volume of the narration. The links at the top of the right pane let you return to previous slides and/or e-mail the author of the presentation. The broadcast is stored on a Web server, where it is accessed by the invited audience. (Our presentation is stored locally, however, because it has not yet been uploaded to the Web.)

A live broadcast, like any presentation, should be rehearsed several times prior to the actual delivery. This is accomplished entirely on a stand-alone computer without having to upload the broadcast pages to the Web. Note, however, that a broadcast contains its own audio, which means that the associated PowerPoint presentation should not contain its own sound files.

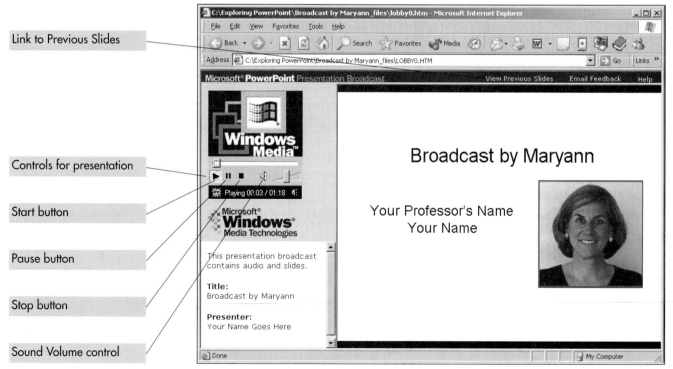

FIGURE 4.8   *Broadcasting a Presentation*

RECORD A BROADCAST

Objective   Create a new presentation by inserting slides from a previous presentation; record a broadcast. Use Figure 4.9 as a guide in doing the exercise.

Step 1:   **Insert the Slides**

➤ Click the **New button** on the Standard toolbar to create a new presentation.

➤ Pull down the **Insert menu**, then click the **Slides from Files command** to display the Slide Finder dialog box in Figure 4.9a. Click the **Browse button** and open the original **Welcome to Computers 101 presentation** from the previous exercise.

➤ Clear the box to keep source formatting. Press and hold the **Ctrl key** as you select the first two slides and click the **Insert button**. Scroll to the last slide and insert it as well.

➤ Close the Slide finder dialog box. Your presentation should now contain four slides; an empty title slide, plus the three slides you just inserted. Delete the initial title slide.

➤ Change the title of the remaining title slide to **Broadcast by Maryann**. Add your name and your professor's name to this title slide. Close the task pane.

➤ Save the presentation as **Broadcast by Maryann**.

New button

Browse button

Selected file

Select first two slides

Clear box to keep source formatting

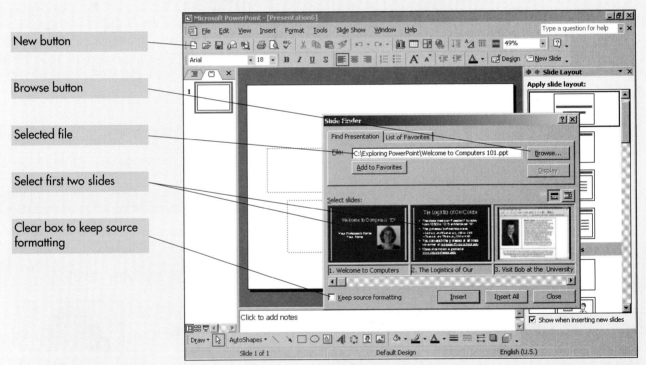

(a) Insert the Slides (step 1)

FIGURE 4.9   *Hands-on Exercise 4*

DELETE THE EXISTING NARRATION

A recorded broadcast contains its own narration and timings. You must begin, therefore, with a presentation that does not contain any prerecorded narration, or else there will be interference with the recorded broadcast.

Step 2: **Record the Broadcast**

➤ There should be three slides in your presentation as shown in Figure 4.9b. The background of the presentation is white, since source formatting was not kept when the slides were inserted in step 1.

➤ Select the first slide. Pull down the **Slide Show menu**, click (or point to) the command for **Online Broadcast**, then click the command to **Record and Save a Broadcast**.

➤ Enter the appropriate information in the Record Presentation Broadcast Dialog box as shown in Figure 4.9b. Click the **Settings button**. Click the option button for **Audio only**.

➤ Enter **C:\Exploring PowerPoint** as the folder in which you will store the broadcast files. Click **OK** to close this dialog box.

➤ Click the **Record button** to begin recording the broadcast. Click **Yes** if you see a message indicating that the broadcast already exists and asking whether you want to replace the existing Web page.

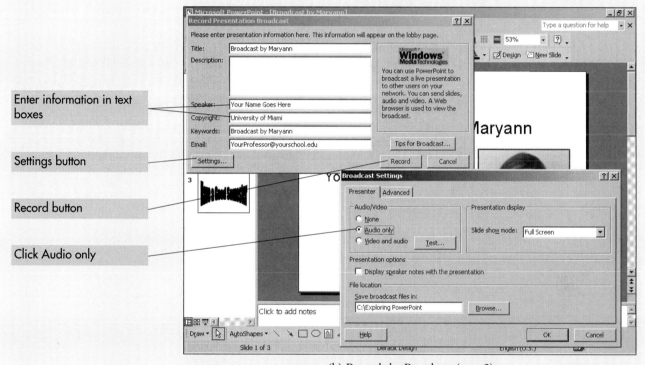

(b) Record the Broadcast (step 2)

FIGURE 4.9 *Hands-on Exercise 4 (continued)*

PLANNING FOR AN ACTUAL BROADCAST

This is an "academic" exercise in the sense that you are recording a broadcast, without actually delivering the broadcast. The latter would require that the broadcast files be saved in a shared folder (a folder that was accessible by others, on either a local area network or a Web server). You might also require the use of Windows Media Server if there were more than 10 people in your intended audience. (Click the Advanced tab in the Broadcast Settings dialog box, then check the appropriate option).

Step 3: **Replay the Broadcast**

➤ Pick up your microphone and click **OK** when you see the Microphone Check dialog box. Click the **Start button** to begin recording. You should see the first slide in your presentation.

➤ Speak naturally and introduce yourself as the instructor as you view the first slide. Click the mouse to move to the next slide.

➤ Continue speaking into the microphone as you move from one slide to the next. Click one final time when you see the black screen ending the slide show to return to PowerPoint.

➤ The system pauses for a few seconds, then you should see a message congratulating you on completing the broadcast and indicating the folder where the broadcast is stored.

➤ Click the **Replay Broadcast button** in the message box to display a screen similar to Figure 4.9c.

➤ Click the **Print button** in Internet Explorer to print this page for your instructor to show that you have successfully created a broadcast.

➤ Click the **Replay Broadcast button** to hear the broadcast you just recorded.

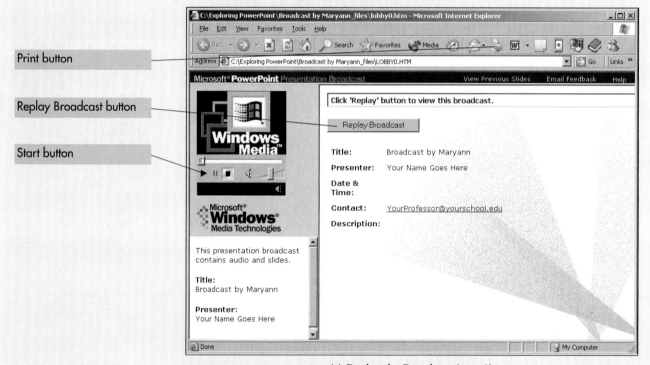

(c) Replay the Broadcast (step 3)

FIGURE 4.9 *Hands-on Exercise 4 (continued)*

SCHEDULE THE BROADCAST

You can schedule a broadcast only if the broadcast files were saved on a shared drive. If so, pull down the Slide Slow Menu, click On Line Broadcast, then click Schedule a Live Broadcast to display the Schedule Presentation Broadcast dialog box. Click the Schedule button to establish the broadcast time and notify your audience by e-mail as to when the presentation will be shown.

Step 4: **Listen to the Broadcast**

> ➤ You should see the first slide in your presentation within the Presentation Broadcast window as shown in Figure 4.9d. The address bar indicates that the presentation is stored locally because it has not yet been uploaded to the Web.
> ➤ The presentation will play automatically, moving from one slide to the next, according to the timings you used when you recorded the broadcast.
> ➤ Listen to the complete broadcast, making notes on any changes you may wish to make. Drag the slider to the left to replay parts of the broadcast as necessary.
> ➤ Experiment with the controls within the broadcast window. You can click the **Pause button** to suspend the broadcast. You can also click the link to **View Previous Slides** to return to a previous slide.
> ➤ Close Internet Explorer. Save the presentation a final time. Close PowerPoint.

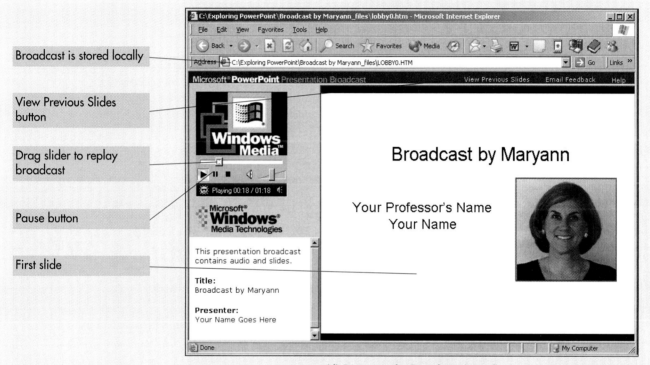

(d) Listen to the Broadcast (step 4)

FIGURE 4.9 *Hands-on Exercise 4 (continued)*

THERE MUST BE AN EASIER WAY

A broadcast is created with a single voiceover narration; i.e., you execute the command to record the broadcast, then you must speak continually from start to finish until you have completed the broadcast. There is no way to stop in the middle, nor is there is a way to replace the narration (sound) for a specific slide without rerecording the entire broadcast; you must rerecord the entire broadcast if you are dissatisfied with a single slide. There must be an easier way, but we could not find it.

Step 5: **View the Broadcast Files**

➤ Click the **Start Button**, click the **All Programs command**, click **Accessories**, then click **Windows Explorer**. Click the **Maximize button** so that Windows Explorer takes the entire desktop as shown in Figure 4.9e.

➤ Click the **Folders button** on the Standard buttons toolbar to toggle the hierarchy on in the left pane. Open the **Exploring PowerPoint folder** on drive C. You should see:

• The **Broadcast by Maryann PowerPoint presentation**; open this document if you want to modify the presentation and/or rerecord the broadcast.

• The **Broadcast by Maryann Web document** that contains the initial page of the broadcast; open this document to replay the broadcast

• The **Broadcast by Maryann Files Folder** that contains the supporting pages for the broadcast

➤ Close Windows Explorer. Congratulations on a job well done. Welcome to online broadcasting!

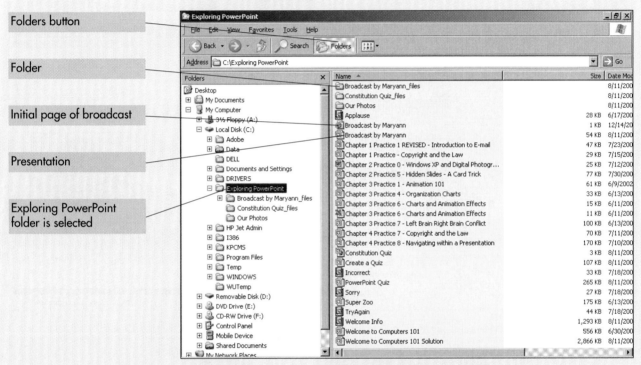

(e) View the Broadcast Files (step 5)

FIGURE 4.9 *Hands-on Exercise 4 (continued)*

CAPTURE THE SCREEN

Prove to your professor that you have completed this exercise by capturing the screen in Figure 4.9e. Press the Print Screen key to capture the screen to the Windows clipboard, start a new Word document, then click the Paste button to copy the contents of the clipboard into the newly created document. Add a sentence or two, describing the various files associated with a PowerPoint broadcast.

The use of sound requires additional hardware, namely, a sound card and speakers. A microphone is necessary to record a sound file, although multiple sounds are supplied within Microsoft Windows as well as Microsoft Office. All sounds are created through the Sound Recorder (a Windows accessory), which creates a WAV file or digitized recording of an actual sound. Sound files are stored just like any other type of file and can be moved and copied from one folder to another.

A template controls every aspect of a presentation's design such as the background, the fonts and formatting of the text, and the size and placement of bullets and other elements. Each template has a default color scheme, consisting of eight balanced colors that are used for the background, text, slide title, shadows, and other accents. Change the template, and you change every aspect of a presentation. Change the color scheme within a template (each template has several alternate color schemes from which to choose), and you retain the overall look, but affect a subtle change in the appearance.

Action buttons build flexibility into a presentation by enabling easy access to the first, previous, next, and/or last slide in a presentation. Hyperlinks to specific slides provide another means of alternate navigation. Hidden slides provide additional flexibility during delivery in that they do not appear during a regular slide show without deliberate action by the presenter.

The slide master enables you to modify the design of a presentation. Select the slide master from the View menu, then change any element on the slide master, and you automatically change that element on every slide in the presentation. The slide master is frequently used to add a unifying element such as a corporate logo and/or action buttons to facilitate navigation during the slide show. You can also fine-tune a presentation by changing its color scheme.

The Save As Web page command converts a PowerPoint presentation to an HTML document, after which it can be uploaded to a Web server, where it can be accessed through an Internet Browser such as Internet Explorer or Netscape Navigator.

The Record Narration command creates a narrative (sound file) for each slide and simultaneously records the time required for that narrative. The narration can be made to play automatically to create a self-running presentation for a trade show or kiosk and/or to embellish a Web-based presentation.

Any presentation, including video and audio, can be delivered as a Web broadcast. The broadcast can be live or recorded. A live broadcast is scheduled at a precise time, and invitations are sent to a designated list of attendees. A recorded broadcast is uploaded to a Web server and configured for on-demand viewing. Either type of broadcast is ideal for reaching large and/or geographically dispersed audiences.

PowerPoint also supports online meetings in addition to Web broadcasts. A broadcast is a one-way connection in which you speak, and the audience listens. An online meeting is a two-way connection in which everyone can communicate with everyone else.

KEY TERMS

Action buttons (p. 178)
Broadcast (p. 207)
Color scheme (p. 178)
Custom show (p. 200)
Hidden slide (p. 178)
HTML (p. 190)
Hyperlink (p. 178)

Insert Hyperlink command (p. 178)
Online meeting (p. 207)
Record Narration command (p. 200)
Save As Web Page command (p. 190)
Set Up Show command (p. 203)

Slide master (p. 180)
Slide Navigator (p. 178)
Sound Recorder (p. 178)
Template (p. 178)
Trigger (p. 184)
Web broadcast (p. 207)
Web page (p. 190)

1. How do you insert a corporate logo or other identifying information on every slide in a presentation?
   (a) Select the object, change to the Slide Sorter view, then paste the object on every slide
   (b) Insert the object on the title slide, then pull down the View menu and specify every slide
   (c) Insert the object on the title and slide masters
   (d) Insert the object on the title and handouts masters

2. Which of the following is true?
   (a) PowerPoint supplies many different templates, but each template has only one color scheme
   (b) PowerPoint supplies many different templates, and each template in turn has multiple color schemes
   (c) You cannot change the template of a presentation once it has been selected
   (d) You cannot change the color scheme of a presentation

3. Which of the following is true?
   (a) A color scheme specifies eight different colors, one color for each element in a presentation
   (b) You can change any color within a color scheme
   (c) A given template may have many different color schemes
   (d) All of the above

4. What happens if you click the Hide Slide button twice in a row?
   (a) The slide is hidden
   (b) The slide is visible
   (c) The slide has the same status as before the button was clicked initially
   (d) The slide has the opposite status as before the button was clicked initially

5. What is the easiest way to switch back and forth between PowerPoint and Internet Explorer, given that both are open?
   (a) Click the appropriate button on the Windows taskbar
   (b) Click the Start button, click Programs, then choose the appropriate program from the displayed list
   (c) Minimize all applications to display the Windows desktop, then double click the icon for the appropriate application
   (d) All of the above are equally convenient

6. Internet Explorer can display a Web page that is stored on:
   (a) A local area network
   (b) A Web server
   (c) Drive A or drive C of a stand-alone PC
   (d) All of the above

7. How do you save a presentation as a Web page?
   (a) Click the Save button on the Standard toolbar
   (b) Pull down the File menu and click the Save As Web Page command
   (c) Both (a) and (b)
   (d) Neither (a) nor (b)

8. Which of the following requires an Internet connection?
   (a) Using Internet Explorer to view the Microsoft home page
   (b) Using Internet Explorer to view a Web page that is stored locally
   (c) Both (a) and (b)
   (d) Neither (a) nor (b)

9. You are using Internet Explorer to view a presentation saved as a Web page when you notice an error. You return to PowerPoint and fix the presentation. Which of the following must you do in order to see the changes in Internet Explorer?
   (a) Save the PowerPoint presentation after the changes have been made
   (b) Click the Refresh button on the Internet Explorer toolbar
   (c) Both (a) and (b) above
   (d) Nothing at all; i.e., the changes will be visible as soon as you return to Internet Explorer

10. A Record Narration command that checks the box to link narrations will:
    (a) Create a separate sound file for each slide in the presentation
    (b) Record the amount of time required to narrate each slide
    (c) Both (a) and (b)
    (d) Neither (a) nor (b)

11. What sound quality and approximate storage requirement was recommended for recording a voice to narrate a presentation?
    (a) CD quality at 172 kb/sec
    (b) Telephone quality at 172 kb/sec
    (c) CD quality at 10 kb/sec
    (d) Telephone quality at 10 kb/sec

12. Which of the following is true?
    (a) You can replace the narration for the entire presentation by executing the Record Narration command a second time
    (b) You delete the narration associated with a specific slide, then use the Sound Recorder to replace the narration for just that slide
    (c) Both (a) and (b)
    (d) Neither (a) nor (b)

13. Which of the following is true about a custom slide show?
    (a) It contains a subset of the slides in a presentation
    (b) There can be only one custom show within a specific presentation
    (c) It must contain narration
    (d) All of the above

14. Which vehicle is best to interact with five of your colleagues in real time to review a PowerPoint presentation?
    (a) A broadcast
    (b) An online meeting
    (c) A Web discussion
    (d) All of the above are equally suitable

15. Which vehicle is best to deliver a live presentation to 100 people?
    (a) A broadcast
    (b) An online meeting
    (c) A Web discussion
    (d) All of the above are equally suitable

ANSWERS

1. c	**6.** d	**11.** d
2. b	**7.** b	**12.** c
3. d	**8.** a	**13.** a
4. c	**9.** c	**14.** b
5. a	**10.** c	**15.** a

BUILDS ON

HANDS-ON
EXERCISE 1
PAGES 181–189

1. A Modified Quiz: The presentation in Figure 4.10 is based on the completed PowerPoint quiz from the first hands-on exercise. The modified presentation contains three additional questions and a slightly modified design. Open the *PowerPoint Quiz Solution* presentation as it existed at the end of the first hands-on exercise and proceed as follows:

   a. Insert three additional slides, each containing a multiple choice question, so that the completed presentation contains a total of nine slides, as opposed to the six slides in the original presentation. You can select questions from the list of multiple choice questions for this chapter and/or you can make up your own. Be sure, however, that the text for the question fits on two lines and that each answer takes only a single line.

   b. Add the appropriate Sound icon next to each choice. Position the icons uniformly from the left edge of the slide.

   c. Modify the slide containing the answer key to reflect the new questions. Include hyperlinks next to each answer to return you to the slide with the corresponding question.

   d. Use the slide master to add a second small crayon at the bottom right of each slide. In addition, delete the large crayon that appears at the upper right of each slide. (You will have to press the Del key multiple times since the crayon comprises multiple ungrouped objects.)

   e. Change the font on the master slide to Arial. In addition, create a shadow effect for the title of each slide.

   f. Restore the color scheme of the presentation to the default color scheme for the Crayons template.

   g. Print the completed presentation for your instructor as follows. Print the title slide as a slide to use as a cover page, then print the entire presentation as audience handouts (6 per page).

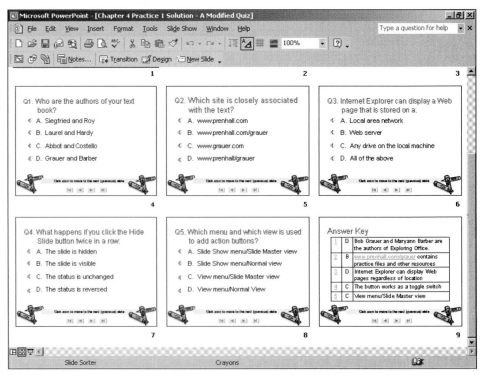

FIGURE 4.10   *A Modified Quiz (Exercise 1)*

BUILDS ON

HANDS-ON
EXERCISE 2
PAGES 192–199

2. Expanded Constitution Quiz: Open the Constitution Quiz solution from the second hands-on exercise. (This is an HTML document so you will need to click the Edit button on the Internet Explorer toolbar to return to PowerPoint.) Proceed as follows:

a. Create three additional multiple choice questions (slides six, seven, and eight) as shown in Figure 4.11. Add the appropriate Sound icon next to each answer to indicate whether the answer is correct or not. Position the icons uniformly from the left edge of the slide.

b. Modify the answer key to reflect the new questions. Include hyperlinks next to each answer to return you to the slide with the corresponding question.

c. Print the completed presentation from PowerPoint for your instructor. Print the title slide as a slide to use as a cover page, then print the entire presentation as audience handouts (6 per page).

d. Open the presentation from Internet Explorer, then print the slide containing the answer key to show that you have successfully created a Web document. Is printing from a browser limited compared to printing from PowerPoint?

e. The Web pages corresponding to this presentation can be viewed locally as was done in the hands-on exercise. What additional steps have to be taken in order to upload the presentation to a Web server? What additional software (if any) is required for uploading? Summarize the procedure to upload your presentation in a short note to your instructor.

f. Explain how to convert the Web page to a recorded broadcast. How do you schedule the broadcast so that it runs at a designated time? Would the sound files and action buttons continue to work in a Web broadcast? Do you need additional software to broadcast the presentation?

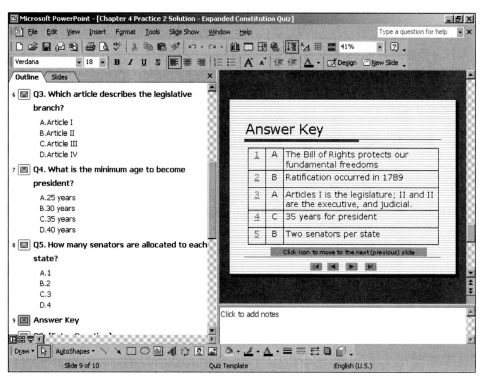

FIGURE 4.11 *Expanded Constitution Quiz (Exercise 2)*

3. Nutrition Quiz: Create a PowerPoint presentation, consisting of at least five multiple choice questions, on any desired topic. Our quiz is on nutrition, and the end result is shown in Figure 4.12. (Slides seven and eight contain two additional questions. Slide nine contains the answer key.) Proceed as follows:

a. Open the *Create a Quiz* presentation in the Exploring PowerPoint folder that was used in the second hands-on exercise. Save the presentation as *Chapter 4 Practice 3 Solution*.

b. Copy the last slide in the presentation (containing the sample question) several times, moving the copied slides to their appropriate place in the presentation. Add the text and suggested answers for each question. Try to keep the questions and answers brief so that they fit attractively on the slide.

c. Add the appropriate sound file next to each answer. Align the icons uniformly from the left edge of the slide.

d. Create the answer key for your quiz with hyperlinks to the corresponding question next to each answer. At least one of your answers should contain a hyperlink to an external Web site.

e. Insert clip art as appropriate next to the individual questions.

f. Change the template and/or the associated color scheme as you see fit. Set a time limit, or else you will spend too much time with your selection.

g. Print the completed presentation for your instructor as follows. Print the title slide as a slide to use as a cover page, then print the entire presentation as audience handouts (6 per page).

h. Save the completed presentation as a Web page. You do not have to upload the presentation to the Web. Print the first slide in the presentation from Internet Explorer to show that you have successfully created a Web document.

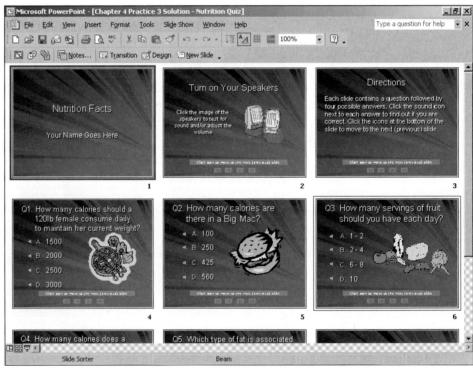

FIGURE 4.12   *Nutrition Quiz (Exercise 3)*

4. Templates and Color Schemes: The ability to include multiple design templates in a single presentation was first introduced in Office XP. Start a new presentation and enter "Templates and Color" as the title of the presentation. Add your name to the title slide in the indicated placeholder. Choose a design template (we selected the Layers design) and add that information to the title slide. Proceed as follows to create the remainder of the presentation.

a. Go to the Slide Sorter view as shown in Figure 4.13, copy the title slide, and then change the color scheme in the second slide. Try to use contrasting color schemes; i.e., light text on a dark background, versus dark text on a light background. Which color scheme do you prefer? What does PowerPoint suggest? (See the tip for new users that appears on the Standard tab within the Edit Color Scheme dialog box.)

b. Copy the original title slide, change to the Blends design, and modify the information in the appropriate placeholder. Duplicate this slide and change the color scheme. Repeat this process at least one additional time, so that your complete presentation has a minimum of six slides.

c. Print the completed presentation as audience handouts (six per page) for your instructor. Use a color printer if possible to appreciate the different color schemes.

d. How many colors comprise a color scheme? How do you change a specific color within a particular color scheme? Be prepared to answer these questions in a class discussion.

e. Search the Web for additional templates that are not provided in Office XP. How much do these templates cost? Are they superior to those provided with Office?

f. Print the title slide as a full slide to use as a cover sheet for this assignment. Include written answers to the various discussion questions and submit the entire assignment to your instructor.

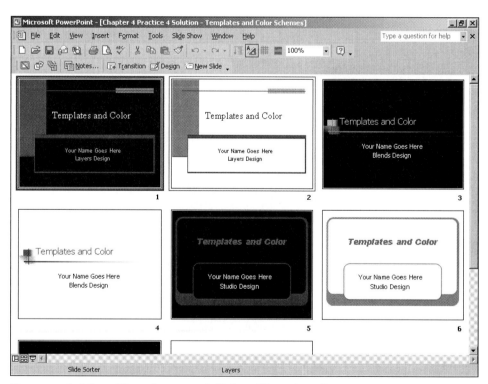

FIGURE 4.13   *Templates and Color (Exercise 4)*

5. Photographs on the Web: Choose any collection of photographs to create a Web-based presentation similar to the one in Figure 4.14. You can select your own pictures, download photographs from the Microsoft Design Gallery, and/or use the photographs we supply in the Exploring PowerPoint folder. Each photograph must be saved as a separate file.

   a. Start a new presentation. Create a title slide containing your name. Insert five or six new slides (choose the title only layout) for the photographs.

   b. Select the second slide in your presentation (the slide that will contain the first photograph). Pull down the Format menu, click Background to display the Background dialog box, click the down arrow in the background fill list box, and choose Fill Effects. Click the Picture tab, click the Select Picture button, insert the desired picture, and apply it to this slide. The photograph should fill the entire slide.

   c. Enter an appropriate title for the picture in the title placeholder, changing the font color and/or the position of the placeholder as necessary in order to read the title.

   d. Repeat steps b and c to insert additional photographs and the associated titles on the remaining slides.

   e. Change to the Slide Sorter view after all of the pictures have been inserted into the presentation. Press and hold the Shift key to select multiple slides, pull down the Slide Show menu, and click the Transition command. Add a transition effect for each slide, which includes the camera sound.

   f. Print the audience handouts (six per page) for your instructor. You must specify color (even if you do not have a color printer) within the Color/Grayscale list box within the Print dialog box in order to see the slide backgrounds.

   g. Save the completed presentation as a Web page as shown in Figure 4.14. You do not have to upload the presentation to the Web. Print the first slide in the presentation from Internet Explorer to show that you have successfully created a Web document.

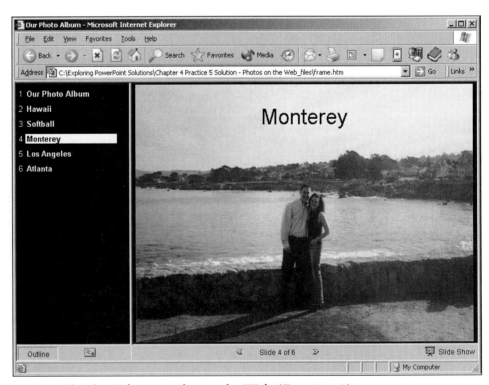

FIGURE 4.14   *Photographs on the Web (Exercise 5)*

6. Brainstorming Session: The presentation in Figure 4.15 was created using the AutoContent Wizard, which provided the design as well as the content. The wizard "jump starts" the creative process by asking you a series of leading questions, then it creates the presentation for you. Proceed as follows:

a. Start PowerPoint, close any open presentations, then pull down the File menu and click the New command. The task pane opens automatically. Select the link to the AutoContent Wizard. Click the Next button when you see the first screen.

b. Select the Brainstorming Session presentation. Click Next. Select the onscreen presentation. Click Next. Enter Brainstorming Session as the title of the presentation. Clear the check boxes that include specific information on each slide. Click Next. Click Finish.

c. The wizard pauses a second, then it creates a presentation similar to Figure 4.15. Delete the third slide in the presentation (overview); the information on this slide is redundant with the agenda slide that is displayed in the figure. Delete the overview bullet on the agenda slide as well.

d. Open the slide master. Use the Textbox tool on the Drawing toolbar to create the text box for the first action button. Create five additional buttons, each of which contains the title of another slide in the presentation.

e. Add the appropriate hyperlink to each of the action buttons you just created. Move and size the action buttons as appropriate. All of the buttons should be the same size and should be a uniform distance from the bottom of the slide.

f. Add your name to the title slide. Print the completed presentation for your instructor as follows. Print the first slide as a slide to use as a cover page. Print the entire presentation as audience handouts (6 per page).

g. How many additional presentations are available from the AutoContent Wizard? Do you see the value of the wizard in jump-starting the creative process?

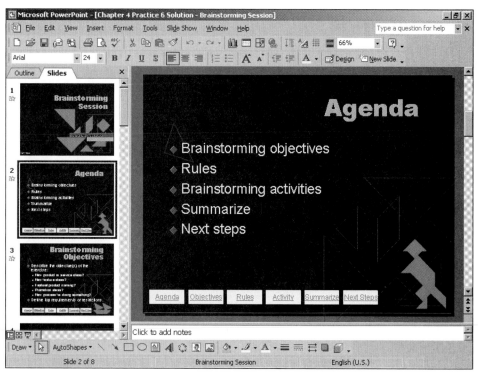

FIGURE 4.15 *Brainstorming Session (Exercise 6)*

7. Copyright and the Law: The 10-slide presentation in Figure 4.16 contains useful information about copyrights and software piracy. Open the partially completed presentation in *Chapter 4 Practice 7*. Add your name to the title slide, then proceed as follows to complete the presentation:

a. Select an appropriate template and a color scheme within that template. (We used default color scheme for the Network template.) Limit the time that you spend searching for a template.

b. Add action buttons to the slide master that go to the first, previous, next, and last slides, respectively. Copy the copyright symbol that appears on the title slide and add it to the slide master as well.

c. Insert the hyperlinks on the last slide so that the displayed text for each link is the Web address of that link. Visit at least one of the Web sites. Did you learn anything about copyright law?

d. Create three custom shows as follows:
  (i) The Basics of Copyright Law (slides 2, 3, and 4)
  (ii) Infringement and Piracy (slides 5, 6, and 9)
  (iii) Using Copyright Material (slides 7 and 8)

e. View each custom show. Press the Esc key at the end of each show to return to PowerPoint. Do the action buttons function differently within a custom show, as opposed to the entire presentation?

f. Print each custom show separately as audience handouts (3 slides per page).

g. Save the completed presentation as a Web page. You do not have to upload the presentation to the Web.

h. Print the first slide in the presentation from Internet Explorer to show that you have successfully created a Web document.

i. Print the title slide as a slide to use as a cover page. Submit all of the printed pages to your instructor.

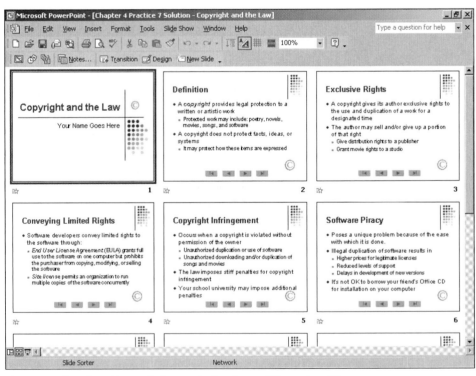

FIGURE 4.16   *Copyright and the Law (Exercise 7)*

8. Navigating within a Presentation: The presentation in Figure 4.17 depicts a different way to navigate through a presentation in which hyperlinks to other slides appear in a menu on the title slide. The hyperlinks are the equivalent of a table of contents as they provide immediate access to every other slide. Open the partially completed presentation in *Chapter 4 Practice 8* (which is based on an earlier exercise in Chapter 1) and proceed as follows.

   a. Switch to the Normal view. Move the placeholders containing the title of the presentation and your name to the top of the title slide. Add a new text box and enter the titles of the other slides in the presentation. The slide titles should appear in two columns within the text box, which was achieved simply by pressing the space bar as appropriate.

   b. Select the title of each slide as it appears on the title slide, pull down the Insert menu, and select the Hyperlink command. Click the icon for a Place in This Document and select the appropriate slide to complete the hyperlink.

   c. The navigation (action) buttons that appear at the bottom of every slide (except the title slide) were created on the slide master. Pull down the View menu, change to the Slide Master, click the Slide Show menu, click Action Buttons, then select the button you want. Click and drag to create the button on the slide master, then supply the necessary link (such as the next or previous slide). Select all four action buttons and size them uniformly. Place the buttons a uniform distance from the bottom of the slide.

   d. Every slide except the title also contains today's date as well as the number of the slide within the presentation. Pull down the View menu, click the Header and Footer command, then complete the associated dialog box to display this information.

   e. Go to the Slide Show view and test the navigation. Print the audience handouts (six per page) of the completed presentation for your instructor. Print the title slide as a full slide to use as a cover page for this assignment.

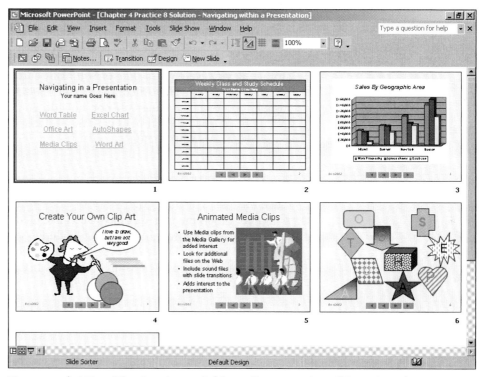

FIGURE 4.17   *Navigating within a Presentation (Exercise 8)*

FTP for Windows

Microsoft Office simplifies the process of uploading a page to a Web server by including a basic FTP (File Transfer Protocol) capability. That is the good news. The bad news is that is that the capability is limited when compared to stand-alone FTP programs. One advantage of the latter is the ability to display the progress of a file transfer. In PowerPoint you click the Save button to upload your presentation, then you wait several seconds (or longer) before the system displays any additional information. An FTP program, however, will display the progress of the file transfer as it takes place.

Use your favorite search engine to locate an FTP program. There are many such programs available, and many permit a free trial period. Locate a specific program, then compare its capabilities to the FTP capability in Office NET. Summarize your findings in a short note to your instructor.

Speech Recognition

Explore the speech recognition capability that is built into Microsoft Office. Use the Help command to distinguish between the Voice Command mode and the Dictation mode. What is the language bar? How do you display or hide this toolbar? How long does it take to train your computer to recognize your voice? What drawbacks, if any, are there to using this feature? Summarize your findings in a short note to your instructor.

Windows Media Player

The Windows Media Player combines the functions of a radio, a CD or DVD player, and an information database into a single program. You can copy selections from a CD to your computer, organize your music by artist and album, and then create a customized playlist to play the music in a specified order. The playlist may include as many songs from as many albums as you like and is limited only by the size of your storage device. The Media Player will also search the Web for audio or video files and play clips from a favorite movie. Is the Media Player (or an equivalent program) installed on your computer? If not, how do you obtain the Media Player and how much does it cost? Experiment with the software, then summarize your findings in a short note to your instructor.

Searching for Sound

Click the Start button on the Windows taskbar to access the Search command, then search for the sound files that have been installed on your machine. (The installation of Microsoft Windows automatically includes several sound files.) Go to the Web (e.g., the Microsoft Design Gallery) to search for and download at least two additional sound files. Describe your experience in a short note to your instructor.